THE *Joy* OF BEING FORGIVEN

THE *Joy* OF BEING FORGIVEN

ANDREW MURRAY

W

WHITAKER
HOUSE

All Scripture quotations are taken from the *King James Version* (KJV) of the Holy Bible.

Editor's note: This book has been edited for the modern reader. Words, expressions, and sentence structure have been updated for clarity and readability.

THE JOY OF BEING FORGIVEN

(originally titled *Have Mercy upon Me;* previously titled *Confession: The Road to Forgiveness*)

ISBN: 0-88368-344-X
Printed in the United States of America
© 1983 by Whitaker House

Whitaker House
30 Hunt Valley Circle
New Kensington, PA 15068

Library of Congress Cataloging-in-Publication Data

Murray, Andrew, 1828–1917.
  The joy of being forgiven / by Andrew Murray.
      p. cm.
  ISBN 0-88368-344-X (pbk.)
  1. Forgiveness—Religious aspects—Christianity—Biblical
teaching.
  2. Bible. O.T. Psalms LI—Criticism, interpretation, etc. I.
Title.
  BS680.F64 M87 2002
  223'.206—dc21

                                          2002001889

1 2 3 4 5 6 7 8 9 10 11 12 / 10 09 08 07 06 05 04 03 02

CONTENTS

INTRODUCTION

*To the chief Musician, A Psalm of David,
when Nathan the prophet came unto him,
after he had gone in to Bathsheba.*
      —Psalm 51:1

I

A Psalm of David for the Chief Musician

The book of Psalms is the innermost sanctuary. It is the Holy Place of the sanctuary of the Bible. In the rest of the Bible we receive instruction from God on the way to draw near to Him. In the Psalms, God opens the door of His secret dwelling place. He shows us how His believing people come to Him, speak with Him, and enjoy fellowship with Him. There we see the throne of grace surrounded with petitioners. There we learn to pray. There the grace of God is manifested in the most glorious way.

Praying with God's Words

To use another analogy, the book of Psalms is like the beginning class of a nursery school. In the more advanced classes, the teacher tells the children what they have to learn. They know how to work independently and need the teacher's help only from time to time. But with the youngest class, who are learning the ABCs, a different method is needed. Every letter must be pronounced and dictated to them. The teacher must put the sounds for the letters in their mouths, until they learn to pronounce and know them for themselves. This is the way the Lord God deals with us in the Psalms. He comes as the Faithful One, nearer to us than in the rest of the Bible. He gives us the very words we need in order to come to Him. He is aware that we do not know how to pray. Therefore, He comes and tells us what we ought to pray for.

When we speak His words, it is with the desire to understand them so that we can feel and pray as He has expressed them. Then He gives us His blessing, and His Spirit makes the words living and powerful in our souls. In these precious psalms, God's Holy Spirit Himself teaches us to pray.

Prayers That Meet Our Needs

This book of the Bible will become more precious to you when you consider the way the Lord God has dictated the words so that you can pray them. Has He sent directions from heaven for prayer as if He had ordained them there for us? If that were the case, they would not be truly human, nor would they be relevant to our situations on the earth. The Holy Spirit has taught us to speak in the language of men, with the feelings of men, and from the hearts of men. The Lord has used men with passions like ours; they are sinners like us, who have experienced every possible condition of human need and sorrow.

God has taught these men by His Holy Spirit to speak these prayers and commit them to writing. Now He offers them to us as a prayer book adapted to our needs. They are adapted to our needs because they come from His Spirit; therefore, they are divine. Yet they are just as human, because they come from those who are our flesh and blood and are in every way like us. For this reason the book of Psalms has been precious to sinners who are concerned about their salvation. Each psalm will also become precious to you if you earnestly desire to seek after God.

In other books of the Bible, much is written about sin and conversion and the conflict of believers. In the book of Psalms, you can see and hear the believers themselves—you have the key to their inner thoughts. You can see them in their fellowship with God. You hear how they confess sin and ask for forgiveness. You can see how they praise God for His grace and pour out their hearts before Him. You can kneel down and pray with them. Your heart will be kindled by their repentance and their faith.

Alone with God in the light of His presence, the writers of the Psalms lay their whole lives before Him. Like looking in a mirror, you can see your life reflected in the concerns, problems, and joys expressed in the Psalms. You can see the hidden conflict coming from the sense of guilt, as well as conversion and faith. You can see what it is like for a soul to be influenced by the working of God's grace.

You will never learn to know sin, especially your own, until you have learned to agree with the deep confession of the writers of the Psalms. Moreover, when you have learned to give praise and thanks with the poets of the Psalms, you will learn to glory in God and rejoice in His grace.

For this reason seekers of salvation have always loved the Psalms. For this reason many of the most distinguished saints of God have said that the Psalms become more precious to them the longer they read and experience their truths.

Think of the Son of God. He taught us to use the Psalms and sanctified them for us. When He was in the heaviest stress of His conflict He cried, *"My God, my God, why hast thou forsaken me?"* (Matt. 27:46). Were these words of the Twenty-second Psalm written to meet His condition? When dying, Jesus cried, *"Father, into thy hands I commend my spirit"* (Luke 23:46). Was that not a word from Psalm 31:5? If Christ Jesus needed the words of the Psalms to comfort and strengthen Him in prayer to His Father, how much more must you and I rely upon these divine prayers to draw near to God?

Praying with the Psalmist

The blessings that come from using these words are abundant. Whenever we take God's words and express them, a way is prepared for the Word to get from the mouth to the heart. *"The word is nigh thee, even in thy mouth, and in thy heart"* (Rom. 10:8). Through the mouth the Word comes into the heart. You will see that the words of God are the living seeds that germinate, shoot out roots, spring upward, and bear fruit. Your heart is the soil. All you have to do is open it. Then you will see that it is the Word of God that works mightily in the believer.

I invite you to meditate with me on the Fifty-first Psalm. Let us learn to pray this psalm. Let us think about it verse by verse. Learn it by heart and receive it into your spirit; then speak it before God on your knees. For David this psalm was the way out of the depths of sin to the joy of forgiveness. It was his way to a rich experience of the grace of God. Psalm 51 can also bring you and me into this blessing, if we use and follow it faithfully. Prepare yourself to memorize and to pray this psalm. The blessings it will bring you are beyond your present comprehension.

II

When Nathan Came to David

To the chief Musician, A Psalm of David, when Nathan the prophet came unto him, after he had gone in to Bathsheba.
—Psalm 51:1

We find different kinds of psalms in the Psalter of David. There are psalms of thanksgiving for praising and thanking the Lord. There are psalms of instruction to teach us one portion or another of divine truth. There are petitioning psalms where God's help is asked for in the midst of distress or sorrow. And there are repentant psalms where, after confession of sin and guilt, request is made for forgiveness and redemption.

Why David Wrote This Psalm

The Fifty-first is one of the seven repentant psalms. Indeed, it is the greatest of them all. To understand this particular psalm, we must pay special attention to the situation David was in when he wrote it. The introduction to this psalm gives us some information. David had deeply fallen into sin. He had committed adultery with Bathsheba, Uriah's wife. Then he had tried to conceal his sin. When he did not succeed, he had Uriah put to death. Even this was not the worst aspect of his situation. If he had really confessed his sin, everything might have worked out. Instead, for a whole year his heart remained hardened. Finally, after the birth of David's child, God sent the prophet Nathan to him, and David realized the true nature of his sin. Nathan had drawn from him a sentence of condemnation against a rich man who had robbed a poor man of his only pet lamb. After David himself condemned the man, Nathan exclaimed, *"Thou art the man"* (2 Sam. 12:7). Then David humbled himself and acknowledged, *"I have sinned against the LORD"* (v. 13).

The prophet spoke to him in the name of God: *"The LORD also hath put away thy sin; thou shalt not die"* (v. 13). This, however, was not enough for David. He was so grieved about what he had done that he went to the Lord in deep humility to confess his sin. David begged God to give him divine grace for the forgiveness of sin and to renew his heart. This psalm was written to confess his sin and express his need for forgiveness.

I want you to understand this psalm because its lessons are of such great value. There are three elements in the spiritual life that we must know if we are to live and die as believers. First, we must know how great our sins are; second, we must know how we can be delivered from our sins; third, we must understand how we should live in thankfulness to God for this deliverance.

These lessons concerning our sinful nature, deliverance, and thankfulness are most clearly explained in this psalm. Let us ask God to open our hearts and impress these lessons on our spirits.

The Magnitude of Our Sins

The first lesson we must learn is how terrible and wretched our sins are. Think for a moment who David was. He was the man after God's own heart. (See Acts 13:22.) He was *"the man who was raised up on high, the anointed of the God of Jacob, and the sweet psalmist of Israel"* (2 Sam. 23:1). Think of the wonderful things God did through him and for him. He had been purified through many difficult trials. God had highly honored him, and David had gloriously praised God.

Yet look what became of him whenever God gave him over to the desires of his own heart. He fell into intense sin and remained hardened in it for a long time. Nothing but the Word of God by the prophet could bring David to his senses.

I am afraid that there are many among us who do not know what their sins are. Until they know their sins, they cannot really come to the confession of their guilt or experience mercy. They will die in their sins. When it is too late—in eternity itself—they will see what sin was. This is the reason I present this psalm to you. I want to show you the sin of David and, like Nathan, say to you, *"Thou art the man"* (2 Sam. 12:7).

I want to show you how corrupt the nature of man is. I want to show you how your heart is the source of all sin and makes you capable of all sin. I especially want to show you how the power of sin can blind a person. You are not aware of your sin until the Spirit of God teaches you to know it. You do not know the real nature, the ugliness, and the curse of sin until God makes it known to you. Therefore, come and listen to the prayer of David, a man of God. You will learn what you still do not know about sin and the misery it brings.

Deliverance from Our Sins

You must also learn what glorious deliverance is available from God. In this psalm you will see that great things must be done in you. David felt that he must be washed by God from his sin, and that his transgressions must be blotted out. He also asked that he be purified within and renewed in his heart; he prayed that the Spirit of God would dwell in him always.

Come with me, and you will hear from David what must take place in you. No matter how sinful and helpless you may feel, you have access in prayer to a God who can and will work in you. David's prayer is designed by the Spirit of God to teach you how you must come to God, and what you can expect and receive from Him.

Gratitude from Our Hearts

You must also learn what it means to live a life of thankfulness to God. You will understand in this psalm how one who is redeemed feels united with God. It is the believer's desire to praise and serve God. It is a joy to tell others what God has done for him. This is not a burden upon him, but a work of love that his heart needs, and that the grace of God makes possible.

Grace will sanctify not only the hidden life of the heart, but also the outward life, conversation, and walk. The redeemed soul is known as one who has become an entirely new person. Therefore, you will also understand how this transformation is brought about by grace and given to a sinner who has the same feelings and problems as you. Yes, in this psalm you will see a man confessing his sin with the deepest sorrow and anxiety. Then, under the working of the grace of God, he receives redemption. Finally, he glorifies God as a redeemed and emancipated soul.

I want you to join me in the study of this psalm, so that you can see how God forgives, saves, and sanctifies souls. You will see how God accomplishes everything you need. You will see that God demands nothing that He does not first give. The service to which He calls you is a blessed, joyful service of willing love. This love is awakened by His love poured out in our hearts by the Holy Spirit. (See Romans 5:5.)

PART ONE

THE GREAT PETITION

Have mercy upon me, O God, according to thy lovingkindness: according unto the multitude of thy tender mercies blot out my transgressions. Wash me thoroughly from mine iniquity, and cleanse me from my sin.

—Psalm 51:1–2

Chapter One

The Mercy of God

Have mercy upon me, O God,
according to thy lovingkindness.
—Psalm 51:1

In this first verse is the key to Psalm 51. During the long period before David was brought to humiliation by the Spirit of God, he could not pray this simple prayer. Only the person who has been brought to an awareness of sin by God Himself is in a position to use this word in prayer with his whole heart. Only the person who prays it from the heart can truly understand it. David learned to pray this prayer on his knees, with a broken heart and in bitter sorrow for his sin. This prayer must be spoken upon the knees with humility and to God. Then it can become a blessing to us, and we can make this psalm our own.

There Is Mercy with God

"Have mercy upon me, O God." We must believe that there is mercy with God. The greatest

wonder of His divine being is that with God there is mercy.

Here on earth we give little thought to this great wonder of God's mercy. However, those in heaven are humbled by the thought of it and never cease to adore and thank God for His mercy. There God is known as the Holy One, and He comes against sin as *"a consuming fire"* (Heb. 12:29). In heaven, sin is known for what it is: the shameful rejection of the Perfect One—a denial of His law and love. It is known that man deserves to be rejected by God. Therefore, it is in this mercy of God that glory is seen.

Angels are amazed that He could have compassion for our fallen race and that He Himself has paid the ransom for our sins at the cost of the blood of His own Son. The idea that He longs after the ungodly, forgives them everything, and receives them as His children is so great that the angels cannot marvel enough over such mercy. David heard that there was mercy with God; therefore, he drew near to Him with this prayer. We also must try to understand and believe that there is mercy with God.

We Need God's Mercy

"Have mercy upon me, O God." We, too, must feel that we need mercy. Mercy is something that is entirely undeserved. David felt that his sin was so shameful, and it made him so guilty in the eyes of the holy God that he deserved to be condemned. It was not God alone who condemned him. He condemned himself. He felt that he was entirely deserving of the judgment of God. His sin

showed how he had withdrawn from God in spite of all the goodness of God toward him. He felt that mercy would be marvelous if he would be considered worthy to be made a friend of God. Yes, the true petitioner felt that he needed mercy. Nothing but free grace could be his hope.

We Must Seek God's Mercy

"Have mercy upon me, O God." We must desire for mercy to be shown to us. David knew that there is mercy, and he felt that he needed mercy, yet this was not enough. He wanted God to show that His mercy was intended for him. He knew that the showing of mercy must be a personal action of God toward each person. "I know that God is merciful," he cried. "The fact that there is mercy for everyone does not satisfy me. I need to know that God is merciful to *me*. Be merciful to me, O God of mercy!"

This longing for mercy is in harmony with what God's Word teaches us on these points. The Word always speaks of *finding* mercy, *obtaining* mercy, *receiving* mercy, *partaking of* mercy, and *having* mercy. From God's side it is called *giving* mercy or *showing* mercy. Sin is a personal offense committed against God. Conversion is coming to God to receive redemption from Him so that He can show mercy to us by taking away sin.

Many people have mistaken ideas about God's mercy. They comfort themselves with the thought that God is merciful. They have, however, no idea how this truth will personally affect them. Mercy must be given to them by God and must be experienced in the soul. They forget that there is a work that mercy does for the soul. They forget that God is the Righteous One as well as the Merciful One. Before His righteousness can liberate a single soul, His holy law must be fulfilled. The sinner must partake of the righteousness of Christ and the acquittal of God. Even with the word of mercy on their lips, many go on to meet destruction. This does not happen because there is no mercy with God for them, but because they have never personally experienced the work of divine grace.

Let us review these thoughts concerning mercy. First of all, remember that there is mercy with God. Let your soul be filled with the thought that with God there is mercy, and that the highest joy of His heart is to show mercy. Furthermore, you need mercy. Without mercy you will be eternally miserable. Especially remember that you must have a personal experience of this mercy. You must have mercy. Without this you cannot rest contentedly. God must do something for you. He must show you mercy. Let God's great mercy and your great misery be the two arguments that cause you to pray this prayer more earnestly. Pray, *"Have mercy upon me, O God, according to thy lovingkindness,"* until you receive God's mercy.

Chapter Two

God Removes Our Sin

According unto the multitude of thy tender
mercies blot out my transgressions.
—Psalm 51:1

In the second half of the first verse, David gave a more precise explanation of what he meant in the beginning of the prayer, *"Have mercy upon me"* (Ps. 51:1). He knew there was something that mercy could and would do for the sinner. It was his desire to experience this precious work. Therefore, he prayed, *"Blot out my transgressions."*

Be Specific

The general prayer for mercy is not enough. The Lord wants us to know and say what we want mercy to do for us. The blind man cried, *"Jesus, thou son of David, have mercy on me"* (Mark 10:47). Jesus called the man to Himself and asked him, *"What wilt thou that I should do unto thee?"* (v. 51). The blind man had already

27

prayed for compassion and mercy, but this was not enough. The Lord wanted a specific statement of what His compassion was to do for him. It is not enough for us to be content with a general request for mercy. The Lord will test the sincerity of our desire for mercy by finding out if we know what we want.

Many people pray for mercy and yet receive no answer. Some think that the first work of mercy is to comfort the heart. This is not so. Later in this psalm, David prayed for comfort and peace. Others believe that the work of mercy consists of changing their hearts and their way of life. Later on David prayed this way, but it did not happen at first. Others suppose they must ask for mercy and trust that it will take them to heaven when they die. They think that in this life they cannot be sure that they have mercy. David taught us that this is what we should ask God to do for us: *"According unto the multitude of thy tender mercies blot out my transgressions."*

God Alone Blots Out Sin

Our transgressions must be blotted out by God Himself. This is the conviction that drew David near to God. He felt that transgressions must be blotted out. He felt that he was not able to do this work himself; mercy had to do it for him. Moses said to God, *"Yet now, if thou wilt forgive their sin—; and if not, blot me, I pray thee, out of thy book which thou hast written"* (Exod. 32:32). Our sins are also written in God's book. The law of God takes into account every sin we commit. In the account book of heaven, they stand against us as a record of our guilt. David knew there could be no fellowship with the holy, righteous God as long as his guilt was not abolished and blotted out. He knew that mercy could not convert or change the sinner. It could not bring him to heaven, unless his guilt was first blotted out. First, the wrath of God must be appeased. Past guilt must be removed. The sinner must have acquittal and forgiveness of his sins. This is the first work of divine grace. Without this, God the holy Judge cannot receive the sinner into His friendship. Therefore, David prayed, *"Have mercy upon me, O God....Blot out my transgressions."*

Many people remain unacquainted with the holiness of God and the dreadful character of sin. They think that if they repent, live better lives, and pray to God, that God, because of these great changes, will receive them. This is not true, although change is good. Rather, you should pray to be changed by the Spirit of God. But this is not enough, because it does not get rid of the old guilt. The fact that you want to get rid of your guilt does not cancel it either with God or man. What you must know before all else is the status of the guilt of your former life. Does it remain in God's book against your name? Is it blotted out? Until we know that it is blotted out, we can have no real peace.

This is why we must pray the prayer, *"Have mercy upon me"* (Ps. 51:1). The blotting out of guilt is absolutely essential. We cannot work this out by our repentance. God has promised to grant it. His promise is, *"I, even I, am he that blotteth out thy transgressions for mine own sake, and will not remember thy sins"* (Isa. 43:25).

29

The Blessings of Forgiveness

This is what the New Testament calls being "justified." In the parable of the Pharisee and the publican, the publican prayed, *"God be merciful to me a sinner"* (Luke 18:13), and he went to his house justified. This was what grace did for him. This was the answer to his prayer, and he went home with forgiveness of his sins. Like David, he could sing when he received this answer to his prayer, *"Blessed is he whose transgression is forgiven, whose sin is covered. Blessed is the man unto whom the LORD imputeth not iniquity"* (Ps. 32:1–2).

Does this seem too wonderful to believe? Remember that the tender mercies of God are very great. It was on God that David called. He prayed, *"According unto the multitude of thy tender mercies."* Come and experience the great, wonderful, and divine element in the grace of God. It will blot out all your guilt at once and remove it completely from God's book. Come and experience the blessing and power of mercy to grant the forgiveness of sins for Jesus' sake.

Chapter Three

Washed in the Blood

Wash me thoroughly from mine iniquity.
—Psalm 51:2

This verse will make the meaning of the preceding chapters clearer. David begged for mercy. He expected the manifestation of it in the forgiveness of his sins. He longed for his transgressions to be blotted out of God's book and taken away from His eyes.

But the sin that he looked at weighed heavily on his soul. It was not only recorded in God's book, but it also had stained his conscience. It clung to him like a blemish that made him detestable in his own eyes. Therefore, he prayed to be freed from the sense of guilt and from this awareness of inner sin.

He knew that this same mercy could erase sin in God's book and in his own conscience. The act of God in heaven is also an act of God in man's own spirit. Therefore, he prayed, *"Wash me thoroughly from mine iniquity."* He knew that the only way his sin could be removed was by a spiritual act of the grace of God. Only this could wash him clean of his sin.

The Symbol of Washing

Why did David use such an expression for the work that he desired to be accomplished by grace? The ceremonial washings and sprinklings of the Old Testament led him to pray this way. Under the old covenant, every priest had to wash himself whenever he offered a sacrifice. Also, any Israelite who had in any way come into contact with something unclean had to be washed first before he could mingle among the people.

David knew that these washings were symbols of what must take place in the heart of man. They were a symbol of cleansing by the blood of Jesus Christ. The New Testament speaks of Jesus as *"him that...washed us from our sins in his own blood"* (Rev. 1:5). Of believers on the earth it says, *"Ye are washed"* (1 Cor. 6:11). Of the redeemed in heaven it says, *"They...have washed their robes, and made them white in the blood of the Lamb"* (Rev. 7:14). In the full light of these expressions let us consider this prayer, *"Wash me thoroughly from mine iniquity."*

The Blood of Jesus

What does it mean to be washed in the blood of Jesus? The Word of God teaches us that the sprinkling of blood under the old covenant was a symbol of cleansing from sin. Everyone who had sinned was guilty of death. But God permitted an Israelite to bring a lamb or another victim to die in his place. Then, when the blood of that victim was shed, it was proof that the punishment of death that the person had deserved had been met. When the blood was sprinkled on the altar, it was accepted by God as valid, and the sin was washed away.

So the blood of Christ was shed as the payment for our sins. We are all under the death sentence. We have sinned and made ourselves guilty according to the law of God. The law has spoken its curse over us as transgressors. It can by no means withdraw its demands until they are met. God would not be righteous if He did not maintain the authority of His law and uphold its power. He would not be a perfect Judge if He welcomed transgressors of His law into favor. Therefore, no one can inherit heaven who is not pronounced clean by the law. And no one can possibly be pronounced clean who has not fulfilled its demands. No person by himself has been able to do this.

Therefore, the mercy of God steps in between us and the law with the gift of His Son. Christ has fulfilled the demands of the law in our place. He was our Representative. He came in our nature to do in our place all that was required of us. He was our Surety, who paid the price in our place. He was the Lord of the law, but He was born under law in order to fulfill its demands. He has honored it by perfect obedience. By dying an accursed death, He subjected Himself to its sentence on our behalf. He has borne our punishment. He has taken its curse upon Himself. Because of that sacrifice, He has paid what He had to demand from us. His blood, His soul, and

His life were poured out in His death. Like the sacrifice, the outpouring and the sprinkling of His blood are the proof that atonement has been made.

You Must Be Washed

You must be washed in that blood. What does this mean? If someone is physically dirty and wants to be cleansed, it does not help to have a stream of water flow past him. If he does not enter into and come in contact with the water, his uncleanliness will not be washed away. So it is with the blood of Christ. You must have a personal part in it. Your soul must come into contact with that holy blood in order to experience the power of it. Christ did not come, as many suppose, to abolish the claim of the law, but *"to fulfil"* it (Matt. 5:17).

The law has a claim upon you, personally and individually, and will ask you if you have obtained the righteousness and atonement of the Lord Jesus. The law will ask, Have you been sprinkled and washed with the blood of Christ? If you have been washed, then you are also acquitted. It is not because the law has no claim upon you, but because it sees that Jesus has fully met that claim for you. If you are not washed in that blood, then it does not help you that Jesus has died.

Fellow sinner, realize what must take place within you, or there is no hope for you. The Lord Jesus still says, *"If I wash thee not, thou hast no part with me"* (John 13:8). With all your praying, seeking, and piety, you will not be saved unless the everlasting God does this spiritual wonder in you—unless you are washed in the blood of Christ. Do not reject the precious blood of Christ any longer. Come to God with the prayer of David, *"Wash me thoroughly from mine iniquity."*

The blood of Jesus has been shed for you, and God Himself is prepared to wash you in that blood. God Himself by the Holy Spirit will bring your soul into spiritual contact with that divine blood. He will make it possible for you to take hold of and experience the power of that blood. It is the work of God. He will do it. Just believe what the Word says. Believe that the blood of Jesus cleanses you from all sin. Believe that without any worthiness in yourself, you can by the attributes of that blood be freed from all your guilt in a moment. Believe that God is sincere when He offers that blood to you. Because of your faith in Jesus' blood, let your prayer become more urgent: *"Wash me thoroughly from mine iniquity."*

> *Being justified freely by his grace through the redemption that is in Christ Jesus: whom God hath set forth to be a propitiation through faith in his blood.*
>
> (Rom. 3:24–25)

Chapter Four

Cleansed from Sin

Cleanse me from my sin.
—Psalm 51:2

D avid's sin weighed heavily on his soul. Three times he cried out before the Lord to free him from his sin. He did not mean deliverance from punishment. He did not mean being restored to God's favor. It was his sin that was so terrible to him. This was what he wanted God to take away. It is obvious that he deeply felt what sin was because the three utterances he used represent sin in a distinct light.

Cleansing according to the Law

First, David saw sin as a transgression of the law of God, a violation of the honor and authority of His King and Lord. Second, he called it *"iniquity,"* according to its inner character, because it was the exact opposite of all that was good, holy, and righteous. Third, he confessed it as *"sin,"* a condition of disobedience and misery. He had prayed that his transgressions would be blotted out of God's book. He wanted to be washed of his iniquity. Once again, in view of his sin, David prayed for cleansing. He made known his desire for the redemption that he expected from God's grace. *"Cleanse me from my sin."*

The word translated *"cleanse"* is the same word that David found in the laws concerning leprosy in Leviticus 13 and 14. It appears there ten times and is translated as "pronounce clean." (See Leviticus 13:6, 13, 17, 23, 28, 34, 37, 59; 14:7, 48.) Let us refer to these passages for the explanation. Whenever someone thought he had leprosy, he had to be brought to the priest. If it was really so, then the priest pronounced him unclean. If it was not this disease, however, then he pronounced him clean.

If a leper had been healed of leprosy, the priest had to pronounce him clean. After that he could return again to the temple and have the enjoyment of all the privileges of the people of God. In the same manner, we see that in the New Testament the word *cleanse* is always used about leprosy. Whenever anyone was cleansed by Jesus, he still had to go to the priest in order to be pronounced clean in the name of God.

Leprosy of the Body and Soul

From these and similar passages it is evident that two things were necessary for cleansing. First, the sufferer had to be clean of his leprosy. Then, he had to be pronounced clean. In this psalm we find these two elements in the purity that is expected from the grace of God. In verse seven we read, *"Purge me with hyssop, and I shall be clean"*; this especially refers to being pronounced clean and acquitted from guilt. Later on, verse ten states, *"Create in me a clean heart, O God"*; this refers to the inner cleansing of the nature and the spirit.

Nevertheless, we see here a distinction between the leprosy of the body and that of the soul. The leper must first be personally clean; then he is pronounced clean. The sinner, on the contrary, is first pronounced clean, and then becomes, more and more, a partaker of the inward cleansing. The distinction, however, is not as marked as it appears. For the sinner is pronounced clean only by virtue of his union with the Lord Jesus. Jesus, the perfectly Pure One, takes him into His purity. Jesus Himself becomes the Guarantee that this purity will be given to him. It is because he is clean in Jesus that he is pronounced clean. Then he becomes more inwardly purified. So the two aspects of purity have one root: namely, the purity of Jesus. The two are one.

The same grace that pronounced a sinner clean also makes him clean. The same repentance that desires acquittal also longs for inward purity. In this prayer, *"Cleanse me from my sin,"* derived from the law concerning leprosy, David appeared to have embraced these two elements together. What he later separated is still united here in this one supreme thought: "I want to be free from sin. Take the sin that I have committed away from me. Take away from me the sin that is still hidden within me. *'Cleanse me from my sin.'"*

It was the work of the priest to cleanse the leper. David wanted to have this priestly action done at the hands of God. He knew that although this cleansing is a hidden, spiritual work, it is nevertheless very real. He knew that no repentance, conversion, or change of spirit or life could cleanse him from sin. He knew that there was only One, the Holy One, who was mightier than sin and was in a position to cleanse him. He knew that this God was *"the God of all grace"* (1 Pet. 5:10) and would do it. Therefore, he prayed, *"Cleanse me from my sin."*

You Need to Be Cleansed

What David found necessary, you also need. He wanted the holy God to stretch out His hand from heaven and touch him and take his sins away from him. Let this also be your prayer. Consider this. "Sin is mine; it is upon me, and it is in me. The purity that God gives can also be mine—both on me and in me. Just as sin is mine, the cleansing must also be mine. Otherwise, I may not be redeemed." Make David's prayer your own. Make your own prayer that of the leper who cried, *"If thou wilt, thou canst make me clean"* (Mark 1:40).

If you find you cannot do this with complete earnestness, think about your sin as David contemplated his. Read in God's Word how terrible the leper's condition was. (See Leviticus 13:45–46.) Separated from his fellowmen, the temple, and the service of God, he had to continually cry out, *"Unclean, unclean"* (v. 45). God ordained this disease as a symbol of sin. Ask God to help you feel what a deadly, terrible disease consumes your soul. As you wander about, away from God's presence and fellowship with Him, pray, *"Cleanse me from my sin."*

And when you pray this way, Jesus will also say to you, *"I will; be thou clean"* (Mark 1:41). The leper whom Jesus healed went out immediately and was cleansed. Only believe in His power to cleanse, His love that seeks you, and His grace that is sealed with His blood. Then you will know that the cleansing that you cannot now understand has taken place within you.

Therefore, let this prayer of David become your own. Your sin, like his, is also very great. For him and also for you, God is the only Helper. Let your prayer, like his, be a cry from the whole heart:

Have mercy upon me, O God....Wash me thoroughly from mine iniquity, and cleanse me from my sin. (Ps. 51:1–2)

PART TWO

THE CONFESSION

For I acknowledge my transgressions: and my sin is ever before me. Against thee, thee only, have I sinned, and done this evil in thy sight: that thou mightest be justified when thou speakest, and be clear when thou judgest. Behold, I was shapen in iniquity, and in sin did my mother conceive me. Behold, thou desirest truth in the inward parts: and in the hidden part thou shalt make me to know wisdom.

—Psalm 51:3–6

Chapter Five

Confess Your Sin

For I acknowledge my transgressions.
—Psalm 51:3

D avid had prayed for mercy and had asked God to blot out his transgressions and to wash him clean from the guilt of sin. He now proceeded to say, *"For I acknowledge my transgressions."* This helps us to understand for what reasons and in what spirit he pleaded for mercy. As one who was guilty, he came to confess his sin. He prayed for grace like one in a sinful condition. Everyone who wants to pray from the depths of his heart the words of David, *"Have mercy upon me, O God"* (Ps. 51:1), should confess that he has sinned.

Acknowledge That You Are a Sinner

This knowledge of sin is necessary preparation for receiving the mercy of God. We can do nothing to cover or take away our sin. Besides, God does not require us to do so. God commands

45

only that we acknowledge the unrighteousness that we have done. God desires nothing but that we acknowledge ourselves to be both guilty and lost. We must fall at His feet and confess the terrible condition sin has placed us in. We must confess that we have sinned and that sin has made us deserving of punishment. We must admit that we are so sinful that we can do nothing to make ourselves acceptable to God. As someone who is guilty and utterly lost, we must submit to God's sentence. We must confess that it would be a wonderful act of divine grace if we were to be received. It is only when we are brought to this point of confessing that we are sinners that we will receive mercy. Then we stand in the presence of God in our true condition. Then we can truthfully honor and praise God for His grace.

Many people do not understand this procedure. They think that a change takes place in their hearts when God is persuaded to show them favor. They suppose that whenever they earnestly repent with a great deal of sorrow and deep conviction, then God will show His grace to them. Therefore, they are always taking great pains to make themselves, in God's presence, as pious and earnest as they possibly can. They think that in this way they will receive revelation and comfort. This is not God's way. God wants nothing from you except to acknowledge your sin and stand before Him as a guilty sinner. Then you will surely and speedily receive His grace. You are to come as a sinner, one who is ungodly; then forgiveness and life will certainly be granted to you.

David's Example

The example of David also makes plain to us man's reluctance to confess his sin. For a long time David was aware that in the matter of Uriah he was guilty of violating the sixth commandment. In the matter of Bathsheba he had violated the seventh commandment. But he acknowledged in Psalm 32 that he had tried to cover and silence his sin. He knew he had sinned, but he did not know how enormous and wicked the sin was. Otherwise, he would have humbled himself immediately. This state of mind lasted for almost a whole year—until he truly realized his sin. When he could no longer hide his evil deeds, he poured them out and acknowledged them in God's presence.

There are many sinners who, in some measure, have a sense of sin. Yet they take pains to forget their sins. They do not intend to sin anymore. With this good resolution they come to God. They think that deeply pondering their sins will make them too discouraged, so they keep themselves back from really acknowledging the depth of them.

The person who wants to receive grace must be willing to look at his sin and think about it. He must become thoroughly acquainted with it. The more thoroughly he makes the bitter confession, *"I acknowledge my transgressions,"* the sooner he will be able to express the sincere prayer for mercy. When he does this, the sooner he will be prepared to receive grace. He will experience what David said after he found that suppressing and covering his sin brought him no rest:

I acknowledged my sin unto thee, and mine iniquity have I not hid. I said, I will confess my transgressions unto the LORD; and thou forgavest the iniquity of my sin.

(Ps. 32:5)

God Alone Reveals Sin

This incident in David's life also teaches us a lesson regarding the knowledge of sin. God Himself must make our sins known to us. It was only after Nathan the prophet had come to David in the name of God with the word of conviction, *"Thou art the man"* (2 Sam. 12:7), that David cried out, *"I have sinned"* (v. 13). By nature, man is so under the power of sin that he can hide it from himself even when he has committed it. This is one of the most dangerous evidences of sin. It blinds the heart. It allows pride to rise and make man unwilling to humble himself. It is the work of God's Spirit to make the soul acknowledge sin.

Many times our consciences make us afraid of punishment, but this fear is the least element in the knowledge of sin. Sometimes trials, sickness, or fear of death make a man tremble with the fear of hell. That fear also is one of the least elements in the knowledge of sin, and a very small indication of the sense of guilt. God may use these things and the fear that they awaken in us as means to arouse a true knowledge of sin. But they are still beneath the level of this knowledge. I have seen many sick and dying men who prayed for mercy without any true knowledge of what sin is.

God alone can give you a knowledge of sin. Pray, therefore, *"Make me to know my transgression and my sin"* (Job 13:23). Let it become your earnest desire to know your sin.

Think about your sin. Confess it before God. Think about it in the light of God's law and Word. Try to think about it as committed against the highest holiness and the eternal love of God. Ask God to send you His Spirit, as He sent Nathan to David, so that you can say, *"I acknowledge my transgressions."* I urge you not to forget that there can be no real prayer for sin if this attitude is not found in the depths of the heart.

My absolute seperation from you God. I Lived the Life of a Sinner No Knowledge or care of your Holy Holy Holy self And how much you Love me

49

Chapter Six

Sin Is a Personal Matter

My sin is ever before me.
—Psalm 51:3

In these words, *"My sin is ever before me,"* David gave a more precise explanation and confirmation of his confession, *"I acknowledge my transgressions"* (Ps. 51:3). He told the Lord what kind of knowledge this was. His sin had made such a deep impression upon him that he could not forget it. It was not just a matter of the understanding. It had seized his heart, so that he could no longer get rid of it. *"My sin is ever before me."*

Sin Is Enduring

"My sin is ever before me." This reminds us of the enduring, abiding character of the sense of sin. A knowledge of sin is not a lesson that has to be learned so that we can forget it again and simply go forward. Instead, it must stay with a person to such an extent that he can never forget

it. Whenever someone confesses his sin and then lives in the world, that is a sign that he is still not in earnest about his knowledge of sin. If he understands his sinfulness—if he sees how shameful and wicked it is—he becomes filled with conviction. He is continually weighed down under the thought of the great evil he has done. This is what we expect from anyone who has done some terrible deed and then gets insight into its character.

Suppose, for example, someone has committed a murder and then obtains repentance for it. Do we expect him to go on laughing or being joyful? Certainly not, especially if the death sentence has been pronounced on him because of his sin. In a similar manner, when a sinner becomes aware of the greatness of his sin, it becomes something he cannot forget, until he is certain that he has forgiveness. He has sinned against God. He has made himself guilty against the law of God and the love of God. In the midst of all his work and the distractions of the world, he states, *"My sin is ever before me."*

This is the great question of his life with which he has to deal. This is the one thought that he dwells on: "I have sinned." Nothing can possibly bring him comfort until God has caused him to know, "Your sin is forgiven." Although one may come to God with all sorts of pious words concerning the compassion of God, the soul still remains in this condition until God Himself takes away and blots out the sin. We should never think that sorrow for sin is unnecessary. We should never seek superficial comfort. Knowledge of sin is necessary, because it is the work of God.

Every soul must learn to say in the prayer for grace, *"My sin is ever before me."*

Sin Is Personal

"My sin is ever before me." This should further remind us of the personal character of a true sense of sin. Those in whom the confession of sin is not deep are always ready to say, "Yes, all men are truly sinners." It is as if the thought of the universality of sin made the guilt of each man less. This consideration tends to divert our thoughts from recognizing the guilt of each particular person.

Further, we imagine there are others who are greater sinners than we are, to whom grace is given. Why should there not be grace for us, too? These are the words of those who are not willing to think much of their own personal sin. They may have some knowledge or some general ideas concerning the greatness of sin, but they do not say, *"My sin is ever before me."* These, however, are the words of the truly repentant sinner.

The one who is truly penitent feels that he personally has to deal with God. He feels that he alone has to deal with God in death, in judgment, and everlasting punishment. It is of little importance whether others join him or not. He sees himself as someone who is condemned and lost in the light of God's law. He truly has neither the time nor the desire to think of others' sins. He cannot ask if the sins of others are greater than his own or not. He finds it sufficient to deal only with himself. *"My sin is ever before me."* He is sincere in his confession: *"My sin."* While many are doing everything to show that the sin

53

is not their own, he acknowledges it with all his heart.

One person imagines that sin belongs to the devil, and that the guilt of it falls on him. Another thinks that guilt rests on the world and is dependent upon circumstances. A third, not in words but in his heart, attributes sin to God, who caused men to be born in this condition. But the truly repentant sinner cries, *"'My sin.'* Yes, more than my property, my house, or my family, the sin is my own/ It is a part of me. No one can take it from me or out of me except God alone." It is a confession of amazing earnestness. *"My sin is ever before me."*

See Yourself as God Sees You

Do you want mercy? Then do not turn away from the painful, humbling side of this confession. Do not consider time or pains too costly in order to make it complete. There will be much you may want to lay aside. But be sure of this: there is nothing that is more important to you than your sin. The first thing God sees in you when He thinks about you or watches your actions is your sin. Since this is true, it is most important that you see yourself as God sees you.

In every prayer for grace that you make, this is what God looks at first: do you truly desire grace and long for it? He wants to see whether you truly hate and condemn yourself as one who is entirely unclean. Do you thoroughly and consistently consider your sins to be wrong?

God looks to see whether you will know as a sinner how to receive and value the redemption that is in Christ Jesus. Therefore, learn this lesson: *"My sin is ever before me."*

Without this there can be no true repentance, no sincere prayer for mercy, no living faith, no well-pleasing fellowship with God. We are destined for the knowledge and the enjoyment of the redemption of God in our lives. In addition, we are destined for heaven where we will be praising and enjoying the free grace that has redeemed us.

I ask you to consider these things because I know that there are many who deal too superficially with the confession of sins. They are willing to confess that they are sinners, for all men are in the same position. But they know nothing of the tremendous importance of this confession. They do not speak about it with shame. They do not pray it before God and on their knees. They say it without really hungering for grace. May God redeem them from their indifference and teach them to cry out with a contrite heart, *"Have mercy upon me, O God....My sin is ever before me"* (Ps. 51:1, 3).

Chapter Seven

Sin Is Committed against God

Against thee, thee only, have I sinned.
—Psalm 51:4

I n this verse David confessed the seriousness of his sin: he had committed it *against God.* As we come to understand this truth, both our knowledge of the real nature of sin and our insight into the reasons why only divine grace can take it away increase.

In order to grasp the weight of our sin, we have to think about how the degree of wickedness of a deed depends on the person against whom it is committed. The same action is considered worse when it is done against a father rather than a servant, or against a king rather than an ordinary subject. This is the seriousness of sin: it has been committed against God.

The Character of God

Who is God? God is the Holy One, the Perfect One, who manifests Himself as *"a consuming fire"* (Heb. 12:29) against all that is evil. He is the King and the Lawgiver of heaven and earth, whose will is joyfully accomplished throughout the whole heaven. He is the Creator and Upholder, who has a right to expect that His creatures will do what He has created them for. He is the God who, in accordance with that right, has given us His law, and toward whom we should show obedience. Against this God you have sinned. That is, you have withheld obedience from Him. You have refused to do what He commanded you to do. You have not hesitated to violate and break His holy law.

You have sinned against Him. You have exalted and chosen your will, unjust and perverse as it is, above His will. You have said that the counsel and the will of Satan is more attractive to you and has more influence on you than the will of God. You have robbed God of His glory. You have opposed Him. You have attacked Him in His honor. You have dishonored this great and infinite God. You, a poor worm of the dust, have confronted and insulted the High and Holy One before whom angels bow down.

And since God is the Lawgiver and the Proprietor of the universe, He cannot endure sin. He must maintain His right in the universe. Every transgression of His law violates that right. The terrible wrath of God is kindled in order to maintain it. Against this God you have sinned. What do you think? Is it not self-evident that the moment a man sees this God in His greatness, this awareness startles and bruises his soul, so that he says, *"'Against thee, thee only, have I sinned'?* Oh, what have I done? I have rebelled against God, the highest perfection. I have dared to provoke His wrath and curse. This <u>God</u>, <u>with-out whom I cannot live</u>, I have made my enemy."

There is one more thought that makes all this more bitter: "The God against whom I have sinned is the God of love. He has not only shown me His goodness in the thousand blessings of this life, but He is also the God of love and the Lord of grace who has revealed His Son Jesus Christ in His eternal glory. And I have been such a child of hell that I have dared to sin against this God. I have despised His Son and turned my back on Him." What an inexpressible bitterness there is for the person who truly feels this when he confesses, *"Against thee, thee only, have I sinned."*

Sin Is against God

The reality that sin is against God is what makes sin so terrible. It is this that makes it so impossible for man to get rid of his sin. Sin is an act of rebellion against the holy God. Man is not in a position to recall this sin or to take it away. Every sin is an assault against God's law and a violation of it. Nothing that man is able to do can possibly erase one single sin that has been committed. Sin has been committed against God. He has observed and noted it. It has attacked Him. He alone can say if He will forgive it. He alone has the power to blot it out and annul it.

Yes, the sin has been committed against God and must be accounted for. Once again, this is the terrible element of sin that is expressed in the confession, *"Against thee, thee only, have I sinned."* Yet how little thought is given to this fact. Even in the case of awakened sinners, they concentrate on the fact that they have sinned against themselves and their own happiness, and they think very little about what should cause them the greatest concern, namely, the fact that they have sinned against God.

Make this a matter of much prayer, because you will have to deal with God. On Judgment Day you will meet Him face-to-face. If you have not thoroughly learned to feel it, then you will experience, to your everlasting horror, what it means to have sinned against God. Even here it is sorrowful and painful to make confession. But it is better to be humbled here than to be condemned forever. Do not allow yourself to be distracted from your attempt to make this confession.

There are thousands of so-called Christians who know nothing of this conviction of sin. Many will say to you that you must not make yourself too anxious about sin, but I feel obligated to tell you that you have reason to worry about your sin. You have sinned against God, and He is *"a consuming fire"* (Heb. 12:29). Your sin is so great, the danger so threatening, that it is highly unreasonable not to be anxious about sin. You have sinned, and God has spoken His sentence of wrath upon you. It is sheer stupidity to look for rest and comfort before you know that God has taken away your sins.

At any moment His anger could explode against you. Hurry to Him with the confession, *"Against thee, thee only, have I sinned."* And if your heart does not feel this truth as deeply as it should, beg Him to work it out in your heart. The Spirit who taught David this word will also teach you to say, *"Against thee, thee only, have I sinned."*

Chapter Eight

God's Judgment against Sin

Against thee, thee only, have I sinned, and done
this evil in thy sight: that thou mightest
be justified when thou speakest, and
be clear when thou judgest.
—Psalm 51:4

David was perfectly sincere in every confession that he made. Under the pressure of what he was feeling, he confirmed, *"Against thee, thee only, have I sinned."* Now there follows another word: *"And done this evil in thy sight: that thou mightest be justified when thou speakest, and be clear when thou judgest."* In these words David presented the reason why he openly admitted his sin. He desired to approve the sentence of God and acknowledge that His verdict concerning him could be nothing except the righteous judgment that he deserved. He had confessed his guilt so that God could be justified in His speaking and clear in His judging. The person who prays sincerely for grace will try to be inspired with this same feeling. Let us look at what this really means.

The Nature of God's Judgment

Consider the terrible nature of God's judgment. Everyone is cursed if he does not continue in the things written for him to do. (See Deuteronomy 27:26.) This is the sentence of the Lawgiver. He explains that every single transgression of His law brings His curse on man. He does not investigate the excuse that man might make. The sentence is not changed. *"The soul that sinneth, it shall die"* (Ezek. 18:20). This word will be spoken to every transgressor on Judgment Day: *"Depart from me, ye cursed, into everlasting fire"* (Matt. 25:41).

The person who is truly aware of his sins admits that this sentence is not too heavy or strict. It is not more than he deserves. He acknowledges that God is perfectly entitled to deal this way with sin and condemn it. However intolerable the judgment of God may be, the sinner feels that it is not too severe. He confesses that he has sinned against God so that he may confirm the truth that God is righteous. This was David's confession. There was no reason for him to plead for any other sentence. If he were still to be received, it must be only by free, undeserved grace. He was, in truth, sincere about his sense of guilt. He must have seen its detestable, inferior nature differently than most men, in order to be able to speak this way. He felt that the sentence of God was something terrible.

In the anguish of his soul, which he had endured for a long time, he had experienced how terrible it feels to be abandoned by God. Yet he acknowledged the righteousness of the sentence and yielded himself to it. This is surely something beyond man's nature. Such a sense of guilt and condemnation must have been formed in him by the Spirit of God.

David Offered No Excuse

This becomes more apparent when we think about man's tendency to excuse himself. David had served God from his youth, and he had suffered more than any other of God's servants for God's name and honor. God Himself testified that David had walked with Him with a perfect heart. At a later time, the Lord allowed it to be stated in His Word that He had strengthened Jerusalem

> *because David did that which was right in the eyes of the LORD, and turned not aside from any thing that he commanded him all the days of his life, save only in the matter of Uriah the Hittite.*
>
> (1 Kings 15:5)

Must this one sin be considered so severely? An earthly king would certainly forgive a single transgression committed by a faithful servant. God, the merciful and gracious One, could also forgive this sin without being asked. There was no necessity for confession.

This is the way that people speak and think. They do not know the terrible reality of God's holiness and His judgment on sin. They do not know that every single sin, although it is only one, is a violation of God's law and an injury to His honor. It is a proof of rebellion in the heart, and it must be avenged. David bowed himself before God, but not merely because God was too strong for him. No, that was not the main reason. David had such a view of the authority of God that he approved of God's sentence. He saw how good it was that the law of God should be maintained and how necessary it was that the glory and honor of God should be established. Under the power of that feeling, he confessed his sin as being committed against God alone. He did this so that he could give honor to God and acknowledge that He was justified in His speaking and clear in His judging.

The Spirit Convinces Us of Sin

Again, this feeling is certainly beyond man's nature. Such a sense of guilt and condemnation had to have been formed in him by the Spirit of God. The Lord has permitted this verse in His Word, so that we may see what happens to a man who is on the way to genuine repentance and conversion. What a different experience this is from the superficial confession of sin with which most people are content! They confess that they are sinners, but they see their sin as a weakness, a flaw in their character, a misfortune. They sympathize with the sinner, but they are unconcerned about the honor of God. The poor sinner must be comforted, but whether or not the honor of God's law is maintained does not concern them.

That is not the kind of repentance the Spirit of God works in the heart. If a person is truly convinced of sin by the Spirit of God, he does not merely think of himself and what concerns him. His great sorrow is that he has dared to commit sin against a holy God, whose law is perfect. His great concern is to restore what he has destroyed. Since he can do nothing else, he falls down at the feet of God and yields to Him the only honor that he can now give. He acknowledges that God is righteous in His judgment.

Have you learned to know your sins? God has given His law to convince you of sin, so *"that every mouth may be stopped, and all the world may become guilty before God"* (Rom. 3:19). Have you already given God this honor, trembling as you did it? Have you humbled yourself before Him as worthy of the judgment of God? Only the person who does this and admits he is a sinner can receive mercy. See to it that you really know and confess your sin. Without this there is no grace. *"Humble yourselves therefore under the mighty hand of God, that he may exalt you in due time"* (1 Pet. 5:6).

Chapter Nine

Our Sinful Nature

*Behold, I was shapen in iniquity, and in sin
did my mother conceive me.*
—Psalm 51:5

David's confession of guilt did not end with the sin against God that he had committed. He realized that his whole nature was completely impure from the time of his birth. From his youth the grace of God had marvelously preserved him from sin. His whole life had been devoted to God's service. But then he suddenly became the prey of temptation and made himself guilty of terrible sin against God. His earlier life of purity could not comfort him; instead, it increased the bitterness of his grief. He felt that his heart must have been terribly corrupted. The power of sin in him must have been greater than he had imagined. Having received so much from God, how could he possibly have sinned like this?

67

Realizing Your True Nature

All at once the root of this sin had come to the surface. For a long time the grace of God had preserved him. He had almost forgotten that he was just as corrupt as everyone else. Now he became aware of his sinful nature, and he came before God with the confession of his inborn corruption. It was not this one sin that called for punishment; rather, "My whole nature is impure!" he cried. "Since sin is always present, I am a sinner who needs God's grace." Or, as David expressed it in Psalm 51, *"Behold, I was shapen in iniquity, and in sin did my mother conceive me."*

The inborn corruptness of our nature is an important element in the true confession of sin. How perverted are the ideas of those who appeal to that fact to excuse their sin! There are many who do this even when they confess their sin. They think that since they are sinful by nature, the guilt of their sin is not as great. They cannot help being sinful, because they were born this way. This is proof that they still know nothing of the real disgust of sin.

Instead, they should be so ashamed of their sinful nature and rebellion toward God that it would embarrass them to remember that they are one with their ancestors in sin. In view of the unity of the whole human race, they would see that God put all of us to the test in Adam. This thought should cause such shame that they would be silent in the dust before God. The confession of this inborn corruption and feeling of shame is a necessary element in the true confession of sin.

Man must come to see himself as God sees him. Man looks only at what is visible to him. When he does not commit many external sins, he thinks that his sinful nature is not as cursed as that of the one who sins openly. David was almost trapped in this error. However, when he sinned, he realized that he had the seeds of all ungodliness in his heart, and that it was grace alone that preserved him from developing these evil seeds. If we truly believe this, then those who have been kept from ungodly ways by a Christian upbringing should present themselves in all sincerity alongside the greatest sinners. They should feel that they are on the same footing as sinners in God's sight. For this reason, the confession of natural corruption is necessary to the true confession of sin.

The Only Solution: Divine Grace

If I have committed only individual sins, then I can try to compensate for them. However, if I am inwardly corrupt, then every attempt to pay for them is useless and vain. Every good effort becomes stained with sin, and I need free, divine forgiveness. Then I realize that I need not only forgiveness of sins, but also renewal of my heart. David united these two blessings in this psalm. As the confession of this inward and outward corruption becomes deeper, the surrender to Jesus and His grace is more complete and abundantly glorified.

It is not just the longing for and reception of grace that depends upon this confession. Greater insight into the plan of divine grace comes from our confession. When I see that my misery has its roots in my kinship to the First Adam, then I see how my new union with the Second Adam (Jesus) redeems me completely from it. When I understand how the fall of Adam destroyed me because I am born of him and receive his life, I learn to understand how the obedience of the Second Adam restores me, because I become one with Him. I am born of Him, and I obtain a part in His life. The all-sufficiency of the divine plan of redemption is made clear to me. I know how to seek my salvation in daily fellowship with the love that flows from God. From every point of view, it is clear that the sincere, repentant person must confess the entire corruption of his nature from birth.

Have you realized and acknowledged this corruption of your nature? Have you learned to see yourself as one who is entirely impure? Do you regard yourself as loathsome in the eyes of God? Do you see yourself as so impure inside that you are good for nothing except to be thrown out?

Are you ashamed of your origin? Does it surprise you that God still loves such an impure creature? Have you turned away from every attempt to improve yourself or make yourself acceptable to God? Do you believe that only God's power is able to renew you? If you feel that you still lack a thorough knowledge of your sin, ask God for it. He can give it to you by His Holy Spirit.

Chapter Ten

Be Honest with God

Behold, thou desirest truth in the inward parts.
—Psalm 51:6

The confession of his sin taught David how to expose its origin. From his birth, his heart had been impure. This led him to think of God as the Searcher of the heart. Before God's eyes, this inward corruption made him worthy of rejection even when he did not openly commit any sinful deeds. He felt that in his confession of sin, he must not leave this truth out. The God he dealt with is a God who desires *"truth in the inward parts."* In our prayer for mercy, it is also important for us not to overlook this word. It will teach us lessons of the greatest importance.

Be Honest with Yourself

God desires *"truth in the inward parts."* This thought calls us to earnest, godly fear in our awareness of sin. By our nature, we dwell more on the outward manifestation of sin than on its hidden source. Whenever the outward life is religious

71

and unblamable because of Christian upbringing or favorable circumstances, many people flatter themselves with the thought that their hearts are also right. They feel that although they still have many sins, their hearts are not quite as bad as has been said. They do not regard themselves as ungodly enemies of God. When God's Word uses such expressions, they feel it could not possibly mean they are like that. If they only knew how the Lord proves and searches the heart, they would think otherwise. The Holy One sees the indwelling corruption of the heart. *"There is none that doeth good, no, not one"* (Ps. 14:3). The holy God requires *"truth in the inward parts."* The service He receives must be completely true and in full agreement with His holy law. Love for God must fill the whole heart. If anything is lacking, then we stand guilty and condemned before God. He cannot be content with less than perfect holiness. This is a terrible thought for the awakened soul. God desires *"truth in the inward parts."*

However, many people experience a superficial conversion and allow themselves to be deceived. For example, there is some anxiety about sin and questions about grace whenever someone is sick, but the person is soon comforted. These feelings of conviction can be easily awakened and also very lightly laid to rest again. Many desire the help of God without being prepared to abandon everything in actual life. *"The heart is deceitful above all things"* (Jer. 17:9). Through the pious appearance of religion, people many times deceive themselves. If they would only realize that God searches the deepest recesses of the soul, then this word of David would be a word of heartbreaking power and at the same time a word of healing and quickening.

God Desires Honesty

"Thou desirest truth in the inward parts." This thought gives hope and comfort to those along the road to forgiveness. God will have nothing less from the convicted soul. The grace of God will require nothing more from the repentant person. I learn to see myself as guilty and worthy of condemnation. In me there dwells *"no good thing"* (Rom. 7:18). How, then, can I arrive at *"truth in the inward parts"*? How can this thought give me comfort?

It comes in these ways: The person who knows himself as lost by nature must present himself to God as he really is. He who comes to God with the acknowledgment of his sin comes in truth. This is the sincerity of which the Word of God speaks. Many imagine that sincerity before God means perfection and sincere dedication of themselves to the service of God. However, the anxious sinner should present himself to God and confess himself to be just what he is. The person who confesses his sin certainly receives mercy. God desires *"truth in the inward parts."* The person who desires forgiveness and is honest with God can rejoice in receiving salvation.

When you appear before God, do not try to present yourself as one who is holy. Do not appear before Him with an attitude of piety. Instead, confess what you think, feel, and do. Hide nothing from the Lord. Do not try to cover up your sin. Acknowledge the whole truth about your sinful condition. God desires truth and will not withhold His grace from you.

Honesty Results in Truth

After we have received mercy, we must continue to be honest with God. God desires *"truth in the inward parts."* The person who has been given grace is aware of the deceit and unfaithfulness of his heart. In faith, love, prayer, and dedication to God's service, he discovers that he is still not capable of serving the Lord with the whole heart and in perfect truth as he desires.

Many times the believer is afraid that his soul will bend under pressure. Then he finds in God's Word this glorious promise: *"I will direct their work in truth, and I will make an everlasting covenant with them"* (Isa. 61:8). He begins to see that this is also a part of God's plan and promise to confirm and bring to perfection the work of grace He has begun. *"Thou desirest truth in the inward parts."* This gives us grounds to plead with God to work out that process in which He delights. This word of David becomes the source of the most glorious expectations.

Beloved, in your use of this psalm and in your fellowship with God, let this verse be the fundamental element of your prayer. Always meet with God as a God who desires *"truth in the inward parts."* In your confession of sin, in your beliefs, in your whole existence let truth in your innermost self be your desire, as it is God's desire.

If you find that there is nothing good in you, that the more you strive after the truth the less you find it, be assured that the acknowledgment of your struggle is already the truth that God desires. If you long for this truth from Him who desires it and who takes delight in giving it, it will be given to you.

Chapter Eleven

The Source of Spiritual Wisdom

*In the hidden part thou shalt make me
to know wisdom.*
—Psalm 51:6

This latter part of verse six appears to be a transition from the confession of sin to the prayer of redemption. God desires *"truth in the inward parts"* (Ps. 51:6). David was led to this thought by the confession of his inborn sin. It was not only his transgression but also his very nature that made him worthy of rejection before God. He could not by nature stand before the holy Searcher of hearts, who desires truth in the very depths of the heart. But this thought led him back to God again, who alone has the power to bestow *"truth in the inward parts."*

God Alone Gives Wisdom

That God cannot be content with less than truth was the very fact that had brought David low; it was also the fact that lifted him up again. If the grace of God received him, then it would give him nothing less than truth. In the hidden parts, God made him to know wisdom.

Here, in the midst of David's prayer, is an expression of the hope that God would make known to him the way to be redeemed from sin. As deep and penetrating as the power of sin had been, so would be his knowledge of grace. He trusted that spiritual insight into the way of redemption would be communicated to him by God.

In this psalm we have already seen the explanation of the washings and sprinkling of the blood of the temple service and the spiritual significance of the Old Testament sacrifices. The connection between the forgiveness of sins and the renewing of the heart is presented in David's prayer as clearly as anywhere else in the Old Testament. His hope was not in vain. *"In the hidden part thou shalt make me to know wisdom."*

This verse teaches us that the true knowledge of the way of grace must be sought from God Himself. He alone can reveal hidden wisdom to us. Human knowledge of grace, which we obtain by the use of our understanding, is not sufficient. This does not imply that this knowledge is not necessary. However, this knowledge is not enough. There is a great lack of this knowledge, even the intelligent understanding of grace.

Knowledge Is Not Enough

Many people have an imperfect idea of what grace is and how it redeems the sinner. They do not understand what the blotting out of transgressions, the washing away of unrighteousness, and the cleansing of sin are. They do not know the terrible nature of sin or comprehend all that is taught in this glorious psalm. It is of supreme importance that clear beliefs be acquired concerning these points. For without real knowledge, faith cannot be understandable, powerful, and joyful. "Do you understand what you read?" is the first question asked by the preacher of the Gospel. "Do you believe with all your heart?" is the second. Such an intelligent understanding of grace is of great value.

However, this is not enough. It is possible that one can have an almost perfect knowledge of God's Word and yet be lost. When we have insight into the way of the truth of God, we still run the risk of becoming content with knowledge alone. When one who is indifferent begins to be earnest and then obtains an insight into God's wonderful redemption, such knowledge sometimes brings him great joy. When he begins to obtain a correct idea of the plan of redemption in Christ, of His atonement, of God's righteousness, and of the new birth, he is filled with admiration and gladness.

Then he runs the great risk of resting in his understanding alone. He recognizes the difference in himself compared to the time when he was indifferent and ignorant. A great change has taken place in him, but it may be that he has not yet experienced an inward spiritual knowledge of redemption. When seeking to understand the way of grace revealed in this psalm, it is very important that we deeply depend upon God. With every verse we must pray, *"Lead me in thy truth, and teach me: for thou art the God of my salvation"* (Ps. 25:5). We should continually use, for example, the prayers of Psalm 25 and Psalm 119 in order to obtain divine instruction of the Spirit in this hidden wisdom.

Depend Solely upon God

It is amazing to think that a person can be occupied with divine truths and yet still be lost. Such an idea could make us completely discouraged. It would indeed do so if we were not able to say in this prayer, *"In the hidden part thou shalt make me to know wisdom."* God gives the wisdom. This is our only security, and it is the only answer we can give to the question, How do we know if we have a right spiritual knowledge of grace? The Lord can and will reassure you of this.

Conversion, or faith, is not a work that you must do. It is not something you can look back on and say, "That was well done." No, the innermost part of conversion and faith consists of coming to God, surrendering to Him, receiving from the *living* God grace to be worked out by Him, and being washed and purified from sin by Him. It is at this point in Christianity that many are so deficient. They do not know that in grace the principal element is coming into contact with the living God and experiencing the power of the Almighty.

True Christianity is a divine and spiritual thing. The whole work from beginning to end is a wonderful work of the Holy Spirit in the soul. The first desire for grace and spiritual wisdom, the *mind* growing sense of sin, faith in the blood of Jesus, *will* and the renewing of the Holy Spirit are all *personality* worked in the soul by God. If you are seeking to walk in the way of grace and to follow in the footsteps of David in this psalm, go to God with every verse. In every confusing experience throw yourself on God. Ask of Him that, step-by-step and word-by-word, He will fulfill this promise in you: *"In the hidden part thou shalt make me to know wisdom."*

PART THREE

THE PRAYER FOR FORGIVENESS

Purge me with hyssop, and I shall be clean: wash me, and I shall be whiter than snow. Make me to hear joy and gladness; that the bones which thou hast broken may rejoice. Hide thy face from my sins, and blot out all mine iniquities.
—Psalm 51:7–9

Chapter Twelve

Claiming Your Cleansing

Purge me with hyssop, and I shall be clean.
—Psalm 51:7

D avid had confessed his sins. Now, the prayer for redemption and cleansing follows. Above all else, David desired for his sins to be forgiven.

In order to understand this verse, we must look at Numbers 19. As many as seven times, we find this word *purify* as the ceremony of cleansing is described in detail.

Whenever anyone touched a dead body, he was considered unclean. Death was the punishment and the curse of sin. Because of this truth, every Israelite who had touched a dead body was considered unclean; therefore, he was not permitted to come to the tabernacle. This external action demonstrated how fellowship with sin and death separates us from God. Only after he had been purified and washed could he be clean again. This ritual is described to us in the nineteenth chapter of Numbers.

A red heifer had to be burned and its ashes kept in reserve. If anyone became unclean, then the ashes were put in water. A bunch of hyssop was dipped in it, and the unclean person sprinkled with it. After he had washed himself with water, he was clean again. Thus he was purified with hyssop.

In the book of Hebrews this ceremony is mentioned as a type of purification by the blood of Jesus. We read in Hebrews 9:13–14:

> *For if the blood of bulls and of goats, and the ashes of an heifer sprinkling the unclean, sanctifieth to the purifying of the flesh: how much more shall the blood of Christ, who through the eternal Spirit offered himself without spot to God, purge your conscience from dead works to serve the living God?*

David already knew that a spiritual purification was represented in this ceremony. He prayed that God might fulfill it in him. He felt that his sin had brought him under the power of death and that he was unprepared to serve the living God until he had first been cleansed by God Himself. The light of the New Testament, especially this word from Hebrews, shows us that this purification can take place only by the blood of Christ. Let us look at what David's prayer, illumined by the Word of God, can teach us.

Cleansing Is Essential

First of all, it teaches us how essential this cleansing is. We read in Numbers 19:20:

But the man that shall be unclean, and shall not purify himself, that soul shall be cut off from among the congregation, because he hath defiled the sanctuary of the LORD.

God is a holy God. Nothing stained with sin can stand before Him. Even a person who merely touched a dead body could not enter into His temple. The impossibility of any fellowship between God and sin is represented under the old covenant by this external strictness. The one who remained in impurity was condemned to death. If he wanted to please God and draw near to Him, he had to allow himself to be purged with hyssop.

God had, in a wonderful way, prepared a sacrifice and water for cleansing. There was no alternative but to be purified with hyssop or to be cast out from the congregation of the Lord. In the New Testament it is no different. God is the Holy One. Sin cannot have fellowship with Him. God is the living God. Death cannot approach Him. Our sins are great, and we cannot blot them out. Even our good works are dead works. They bear in themselves the token of sin and the death of the corrupt nature from which they come. The person who is not purified in the way appointed by God, through the Sacrifice commanded by Him, will be cut off from the congregation.

Nothing you can do, nor any change you make, can restore your access to God. Only one thing is necessary: you must be cleansed by God

Himself. Otherwise you will not enter His heaven. Let this prayer of David become your own: *"Purge me with hyssop, and I shall be clean."*

Cleansing Is Available

David's prayer teaches us that this purifying is available to us. The Spirit of God taught David to pray in harmony with what the temple services taught. The New Testament says to us, *"How much more shall the blood of Christ...purge your conscience from dead works to serve the living God?"* (Heb. 9:14). Yes, it is the blood of Christ that can cleanse us. The red heifer was killed and burned. Its blood was sprinkled on the tabernacle. Yet the water of purification made from the ashes of this sacrifice could not truly cleanse anyone.

Jesus is the perfect Sacrifice. He died for our sins. He has overcome the power of sin and of death and made sin powerless. He has entered with His blood into the Holy Place. You also can be purified and cleansed. Draw near to God with the humble prayer that He will purge you, sprinkle you with this blood, and cause you to experience the power of it. He will do it. The blood of Jesus will cleanse you from all sin (1 John 1:7).

If by faith you seek to appropriate His blood, the Spirit of God will give you the assurance that God has taken away all your sin. Go to the fountain of Jesus' blood. Praying, watching, and trusting, present yourself to God. By faith you will know that you are clean.

You will know that you are pure. Your heart will not be so holy that you cannot commit sin anymore, but it will be so purified by the blood that sin is no longer accounted to you. You are no longer burdened with it. You are so purified by the Spirit, which is imparted with the blood, that you have a clean heart on which the law of God is written and lives. Jesus said to His disciples, *"He that is washed needeth not save to wash his feet, but is clean every whit: and ye are clean"* (John 13:10).

Let David's prayer become your own. *"Purge me...and I shall be clean."* The more earnestly you express that first word with your eyes on Jesus, *"Purge me,"* the more powerfully the Spirit of God will also apply that second word to you, *"I shall be clean."*

Chapter Thirteen

Perfectly Purified

Wash me, and I shall be whiter than snow.
—Psalm 51:7

The prayer to be washed, which we read in verse two, is repeated once more. This time an explanation of great importance is added to it. David said to the Lord what he believed the wonderful power of that washing would be, *"Wash me, and I shall be whiter than snow."* Many people who pray the prayer for grace and forgiveness do not know the answer they ought to expect. They do not believe that the prayer will be gloriously heard. They do not believe that they will be able to draw near to God with the absolute certainty of being *"whiter than snow."*

In order to understand this prayer thoroughly, we must look at this phrase, *"whiter than snow."* It does not refer to the inward renewal and purifying of the heart. David did not say that when he was washed he would be perfect and would never commit sin. The person who has been washed clean may always fall again into the mire and become soiled. Grace gives an inward purity. It does not come at once in perfect form, but gradually, step-by-step.

David spoke about this later when he prayed for a clean heart. What he spoke about here is the freedom from guilt that everyone receives with the forgiveness of sins. When God forgives sins, He forgives at once and perfectly. At the moment when God forgives sins, the soul, in His eyes and according to His holy law, is without a spot and is entirely clean. As Jesus said to Peter, *"He that is washed...is clean every whit"* (John 13:10). Or as David said, he is *"whiter than snow."*

Purified for Heaven

"Wash me, and I shall be whiter than snow." Every one of us should make this prayer his own. There are some strong arguments that will urge you to take this step. Nothing less than this can keep you pure. You will not be satisfied with less. We have said before that the law of God stands at the gate of heaven and guards the entrance to it. It does not let anyone in who is not *"whiter than snow."*

That is the holiness of God and the perfection of the angels. Anything that is less clean and less holy is not permitted in heaven. If there is one single stain in you, the law will reject you. All heaven will throw you out. On Judgment Day, when God's justice flashes out to consume in fire everything stained with sin, nothing that is not *"whiter than snow"* will stand before a holy God.

Purified Perfectly

Furthermore, nothing less than perfect purification is offered to you. If you had to purify yourself, you would soon lose hope. God says, *"For though thou wash thee with nitre, and take thee much soap, yet thine iniquity is marked before me"* (Jer. 2:22). Instead of this, God has prepared all that is necessary for your salvation. When God forgives, He forgives perfectly. *"As far as the east is from the west, so far hath he removed our transgressions from us"* (Ps. 103:12).

The washing of the soul is God's work, an act of God's holy and all-prevailing grace. He is in a position to make us *"whiter than snow."* It is the blood of Jesus in which we are washed. The power of divine holiness, found in that precious atoning blood, has the power to make us *"whiter than snow."*

In other words, the atonement of Jesus Christ is perfect. His righteousness is perfect. His merit is infinite. If His righteousness is attributed to me, I obtain it perfectly and entirely. If I have a part in the Lord Jesus, my Surety, then I have Him completely. Christ is not divided. I am in Him. I have His full righteousness, or I am not in Him and have no part in it. When Jesus bore the curse with us, it was not attributed to Him and laid upon Him according to the measure of His merit and worthiness. It was according to ours. Before God we are endowed with grace along with Jesus. His righteousness is bestowed on us, not according to our merit, but according to that of Jesus. It was an act of divine righteousness that Jesus came as a man to take our full curse on Himself. In like manner, it is an act of God's righteousness that we can come to Him in Jesus to take for ourselves the complete righteousness of Jesus.

Jesus is identified with us as One upon whom the curse must rest. He who believes in Him is one with Jesus and is treated as such. He is accepted in Him and is *"whiter than snow."* God sees us in Christ. Our sins are entirely and completely forgiven. We are altogether acceptable to Him. He fulfills to us the word, *"Though your sins be as scarlet, they shall be as white as snow; though they be red like crimson, they shall be as wool"* (Isa. 1:18). Therefore, let everyone pray, *"Wash me, and I shall be whiter than snow."* God has offered us nothing less than this.

The Blessings of Being Purified

Nothing less than this purifying can bring full peace. Many seek peace with God in their own activities, endeavors, and experiences, but they cannot find stable, full peace—the peace that Jesus gives and that passes *"all under-standing"* (Phil. 4:7). Only when we can speak these words by faith, "I shall be clean; I shall be whiter than snow," do we know what it means to say, *"Blessed is he whose transgression is forgiven, whose sin is covered"* (Ps. 32:1). Only then do we know what is meant by singing, *"Bless the LORD, O my soul,...who forgiveth all thine iniquities"* (Ps. 103:2–3). Then our consciences can obtain full peace in view of God and sin, law and the curse, and death and judgment. This happens because the blood of Jesus makes us *"whiter than* snow." The soul rejoices with a joy that is "*un-speakable and full of glory*" (1 Pet. 1:8).

Nothing less than this must be your desire. Lay aside your own prayers and thoughts about what God is to do for you. Learn to pray as the Holy Spirit taught David, *"Wash me, and I shall be whiter than snow."* Keep these words in your heart. Speak them continually before God in prayer. Make them your continual desire. You will obtain a richer blessing than your prayers have brought you for years.

Receive this blessing by faith. This grace is offered to you in Christ. Believe that through Him this purification is prepared for you. Believe in Him, and you will not only ask with confidence, but also firmly believe that God is doing it: "He washes me, and I am whiter than snow." Draw near to Him and take the blessing out of His hand.

Chapter Fourteen

The Joy of Being Broken

Make me to hear joy and gladness; that the
bones which thou hast broken may rejoice.
—Psalm 51:8

D avid did not simply long for forgiveness;
he desired more. He wanted joy, gladness,
and rejoicing. To him this was a portion of
the grace that he asked for. If this grace is to be
full and free, then he expected that it would fill
his heart with gladness.

Many people concerned about salvation do
not understand David's request. They think that
it is too large a blessing to desire from God, that
they are too unworthy to expect to receive such
deep joy from God. They are content to be miserable and depressed all their lives, as long as they
can hang onto the hope of one day getting to
heaven. They feel too unworthy to ask for joy and
gladness on earth as well. They think they are
not fit to expect such a blessing, and they call
this attitude humility. No, in truth, they are always wanting to measure grace according to
their own merits, and that is not real grace!

The Joy of Forgiveness

David gave us the example of how we are to know God better, and how to cherish the riches of His grace. He knew that when God forgives, He forgives completely. When He receives anyone again, He receives him with His whole heart. The Lord does not want any cloud separating Him and the believing soul. He wants that person to know that he is completely restored to His favor. He is restored as completely as if he had never committed sin and can now rejoice with confidence in the forgiving love of God. David knew this. Although he had fallen amazingly low, he was not afraid to ask for entire restoration to the love of God when he asked for grace. *"Make me to hear joy and gladness; that the bones which thou hast broken may rejoice."*

Everyone who studies this psalm should understand that he is entitled to ask for nothing less than joy and gladness. God desires this on the part of His people. *"Rejoice in the Lord alway: and again I say, Rejoice"* (Phil. 4:4). Jesus also desires it. *"These things have I spoken unto you, that my joy might remain in you, and that your joy might be full"* (John 15:11). The nature of the case, the glory of the reward, and the love and goodness of God all entitle us to expect that forgiveness will transmit joy.

And if we would understand what this joy and gladness consists in, an explanation is readily given: it is in receiving what David had prayed for—the cleansing of his sins. Yes, it was from the forgiveness of his sins that he expected such gladness. It was always the sense of his sin that had grieved and pained him terribly. As long as he had no certainty concerning this blessing, he could have no peace. But when David knew that God was reconciled to him and that his sins were blotted out of God's book; when he knew that he was washed whiter than snow and thus restored to God's favor, no wonder he expected his heart to be filled with joy and gladness! Because of this knowledge, David prayed that the word of forgiveness spoken to his soul would cause him to *"hear joy and gladness."*

How different this attitude is from those who pray for a short time, then seek their joy in the world because they know nothing of the joy of God. How different it is from those who pray for forgiveness but do not believe that this blessing can fill them with joy. How different it is from those who seek the fountain of joy only in themselves or in some wonderful change of heart or holiness in their lives. Learn from David that at the very moment you come to the blood of Jesus to receive forgiveness, you can be filled with the joy of God. *"Blessed is he whose transgression is forgiven, whose sin is covered"* (Ps. 32:1). To the sinner Jesus says, *"Be of good cheer; thy sins be forgiven thee"* (Matt. 9:2).

Brokenness Brings Joy

But why is it that so many never receive this gladness? The eighth verse of Psalm 51 points out the true reason. When David said, *"That the bones which thou hast broken may rejoice,"* he reminded us how terrible his conviction of sin was. God had bruised him. He felt that God was his enemy, that God's wrath was upon him, and that he could not resist God or even stand before

97

Him. The curse of God's law struck him down, and he lay bruised in the dust.

The reality of sin and the astonishing nature of God's wrath bruised him to such an extent that there was no healing. Now nothing could possibly comfort him unless he received complete forgiveness and restoration. If there was the least doubt at this point, he could no longer rest. Was God's forgiveness a reality for him? He wanted to be assured of this by hearing God's voice of joy and gladness.

This is the reason why so many never come to the joy of God and never earnestly long for it. They have never truly felt the weight of their sins. They cannot speak to God of *"the bones which thou hast broken."* They know that they are sinners, but the conviction is simply a thing of the understanding. The fear of the Lord is never upon them. They have never been moved by the sense of God's wrath. They do not feel that it is a terrible thing *"to fall into the hands of the living God"* (Heb. 10:31). The Spirit has not convinced them of sin. They have never learned to cry out, *"Woe is me! for I am undone"* (Isa. 6:5). Therefore, they feel little need for joy and the certainty of God's forgiving love.

Lord, pour out Your Holy Spirit so that many will know their sins and feel real anxiety in their souls. Let the law bruise them and the curse terrify them. Let the Cross break them down so that they can find no rest until they find forgiveness and the joy of God in the blood of the Cross.

Chapter Fifteen

Your Sins Are Hidden

Hide thy face from my sins.
—Psalm 51:9

In this verse, David expressed in a new way what he wanted the grace of God to do for him. He expected God to hide His face from his sin and not see it anymore. This was also one aim in the prayer that opens Psalm 51, *"Have mercy upon me, O God."*

Our Sins Are before God

This blessing is in total agreement with what the Word of God teaches us. As long as our sins are not forgiven, they stand before the face of God in order to accuse us. He hears the accusation that they bring against us. He looks at them in all their wickedness as a transgression of His law, and they awake His anger and disapproval. God's Word says, *"Thou hast set our iniquities before thee, our secret sins in the light of thy countenance"* (Ps. 90:8). And Jeremiah 2:22 says, *"For though thou wash thee with nitre, and take thee much soap, yet thine iniquity is marked before me, saith the Lord GOD."*

In David's bitter experience, this thought became a terrible truth. He felt not only what he confessed, *"My sin is ever before me"* (Ps. 51:3), but also what is more terrible, that his sin was ever before God. He saw his sins, and he was terrified. But he also said that God saw them (v. 4). Every sin he had committed was there before the face of God.

May God grant that each of us would feel this same truth. Then perhaps we will be able to understand the glory of David's prayer. We will then feel that every sin, as soon as it is committed, goes to lengthen the list of our accusers before the face of God. Once a sin is committed, it is no longer in man's power. We cannot recall or annul it. No repentance, tears, or promise of new obedience can cover it or take it away. Only an act of God's free grace can give us the blessed certainty that our sin is no longer before God's face.

Our Sins Are Hidden from God

What is this act of God? In our text, David called it, *"Hide thy face from my sins."* To hide one's face from anything means not to see it. David's prayer is the same as what is said elsewhere in the Scriptures. For example, Numbers 23:21 says, *"He hath not beheld iniquity in Jacob, neither hath he seen perverseness in Israel."* Similarly, Hezekiah prayed, *"But thou hast in love to my soul delivered it from the pit of corruption:*

for thou hast cast all my sins be
(Isa. 38:17). The prophet Micah
turn again, he will have compassion
will subdue our iniquities; and thou
their sins into the depths of the sea" (I.
In a similar manner, the Lord spoke   ...ne
prophet Jeremiah:

> *In those days, and in that time, saith the*
> LORD, *the iniquity of Israel shall be sought*
> *for, and there shall be none;...for I will*
> *pardon them whom I reserve.*   (Jer. 50:20)

These words of Scripture help us to understand the forgiveness of God. He casts our sins behind His back. He throws them into the depths of the sea so that they can never be found. He turns His face from them and sees them no more.

This is blessedness, to know that our sins are forgiven. Christ has reduced them to nothing. Our sins can no longer stand against us. The face of God that was turned away from our sins is now turned toward us in favor. God no longer sees our sin in anger. He looks at us in mercy. This is nothing different from what the New Testament calls justification. When the sinner is released from his sins, then he is a justified soul in the eyes of God. His former sins are no longer found. God has hidden His face from them. When the holy Judge no longer sees them, then the acquitted soul can rejoice in the assurance of His favor and love.

At this point, however, someone may ask, How can the omniscient, faithful God, who knows my sins, shut His eyes to them and not notice them? He is always the perfectly Righteous One. It is impossible for Him to look upon sin and pretend not to see it. When God turns His eyes from your sins, hides His face, and casts your sins behind His back, He does this because satisfaction for them has been made through Jesus.

When God receives from Jesus the assurance that you belong to Him and have a part in the annulling of guilt by His blood, then He no longer has to deal with your sins. They have been put away. Then it is precisely His righteousness that demands that He should no longer remember your sins but hide His face from them. As long as your sins are before Him, God must look at them. But when they are charged to Jesus, with the satisfaction of Him as your payment, God cannot look at them anymore. They have been accounted for and put away.

Look to Jesus

We also learn in what spirit you are to make David's prayer, *"Hide thy face from my sins,"* your own. Look at the Lord Jesus when He bore your sins to the cross and annulled the guilt of them. Look at Him with the complete atonement that He brought about and offered to you by God. Look at Him as given for you by God so that you can receive Him with confidence and come to God in Him.

Yes, look at Him as waiting for you. Look at Him until your faith comes alive and you can say, "Jesus is also for me. God hides His face from my sins. *'Thou hast cast all my sins behind thy back'* (Isa. 38:17)."

This is a matter of great concern and amazing interest. All your sins are before the face of God. They cry out for vengeance. Day and night their cry ascends to God: "This sinner has angered You. He is worthy of the curse. O holy God, do not hide Your face from his sins." The law of God supports their plea: "O holy God, he has transgressed Your law. Do not hide Your face from his sins." The sinner who must experience this is distressed. For this reason, let your prayer go up to God, *"Hide thy face from my sins."* Plead the promise of God and the blood of Jesus. Ask Jesus to become your Intercessor. You will see that God hears this prayer. The blood of Jesus has great power. He is in a position to cover your sins and to take them away from before God.

Chapter Sixteen

Receiving Forgiveness

Blot out all mine iniquities.
—Psalm 51:9

Here this prayer is heard for the second time in this psalm. It was the first word David used after he had begun to pray for mercy, in order to say what he desired from this mercy. He had already expressed his desires by other expressions, such as *"wash me"* (v. 2), *"cleanse me"* (v. 2), *"purge me"* (v. 7), *"make me to hear joy and gladness"* (v. 8), and *"hide thy face from my sins"* (v. 9). Once more, he gathered all his requests together in these significant words, *"Blot out all mine iniquities."*

For an explanation of this statement, we refer to what has already been said in verse one. It is important for us to use this word to reflect on the preceding portion of the psalm. Also, this is the last time this point is referred to in the psalm. In the following three verses, David asked for an inward renewal of his heart by the Spirit of

God. And from verse thirteen to the end of the psalm, he spoke of the fruits of thanksgiving that God's redemption brings.

Understanding Forgiveness

Yet before proceeding in this manner, David once again repeated the prayer, *"Blot out all mine iniquities."* In this way he showed us that he was sincere about this matter. He knew that forgiveness was the root and beginning of all the rest. If there is no clear understanding between God and the sinner regarding the forgiveness of sins, there can be no further question about a new life. Therefore, friend, I will also deal with you on this matter earnestly, definitely, and with all sincerity. I want to ask you some questions concerning this all-important matter.

Do you thoroughly understand what the forgiveness of sins—the blotting out of iniquities—is? There are many earnest Christians who do not thoroughly understand that this is the foundation of our redemption. Do you understand that the blotting out of all sins is the first blessing God wants to give to the one who longs to be saved? Do you understand that God is prepared to give it immediately to everyone who receives it trustfully?

God offers forgiveness to us continually. Do you understand that if you sincerely take the Savior with His blood, you can receive it as a gift of God? Along with Jesus you actually receive, by faith, the blotting out of your sins. Do you know that by faith you can know that your sins are blotted out of God's book? The Holy Spirit, as the

Spirit of faith, bears witness to you of this forgiveness.

Do you understand that this blotting out is perfect and complete? Your soul appears before God *"whiter than snow"* (Ps. 51:7) and can look to God as a God who is no longer angry with you. Do you understand all this, or is it still unclear to you? When we talk about these things, do you feel like someone who is still groping in the dark? See that you come to a clear understanding of these points, my friend, because your salvation depends on it.

Seeking Forgiveness

Are you really seeking forgiveness and the blotting out of your sins? I am not asking if you know that you need to be saved, if you are sometimes troubled, if you occasionally pray, or if you pray every day, *"Forgive us our sins"* (Luke 11:4). In the presence of God, the Searcher of hearts, can you say that you are known to Him as one who really seeks forgiveness? Can God declare that you are hungering and thirsting for it?

Can you say that day by day you are seeking and striving for this grace as something that is of vital importance? Have you given up sin and forsaken the world to obtain this forgiveness? And are you earnestly pleading before God to give it to you as the one blessing that He has to give you?

Yes, are you really seeking it in church, in God's Word, in your prayer time, as the one thing for which you are willing to consider everything as loss? It is worth seeking. God wants us to seek it. Only he who seeks it with all his heart will obtain it. Are you really seeking it this way?

Praying for Forgiveness

I have another question. If you have not been seeking this blotting out of your sins, or you have only begun desiring to seek it, this question does not concern you. But if you have been seeking forgiveness, have you found it? Are your sins forgiven? Do you know, as surely and truly as the guilt of your sin was upon you, that you are now clean in God's sight because He has blotted out all your sins? I know that many shrink from these questions, but it is for that reason that I ask them.

When David prayed for mercy, he was not content with indefinite ideas about the goodness of God. No, he knew what goodness wanted to do for him. He expected it to do something real for him. He prayed for the blotting out of his sins with the hope of obtaining an answer to that prayer. He also prayed in the hope that the joy and power of a new life would be fulfilled in him, as he so often sang of in later psalms. For example, in Psalm 103:2–3, he said, *"Bless the LORD, O my soul,...who forgiveth all thine iniquities."*

Therefore, I ask you, are your sins blotted out? If this is not the case, then you are not where you ought to be. You still do not have a part in God's salvation. I say to you, "Hurry to God." Do not remain standing far off. Pray and believe. This blessing really can be found. This blessing is for each of us; it is for you! Sin can be destroyed.

Let your whole soul become fixed on this one aim—the blotting out of your sin. Without this blessing there is no salvation. Only God can give it. He desires to give it. He will give it. God will perform this divine deed for you. He will take away all your sins. Just let this prayer be heard from the depths of your heart, *"Blot out all mine iniquities."* Let faith look on Christ. The Son of God can save sinners. He who believes in Him will not be ashamed (Rom. 9:33).

PART FOUR

THE PRAYER FOR RENEWAL

Create in me a clean heart, O God; and renew a right spirit within me. Cast me not away from thy presence; and take not thy holy spirit from me. Restore unto me the joy of thy salvation; and uphold me with thy free spirit.

—Psalm 51:10–12

Chapter Seventeen

A Clean Heart

Create in me a clean heart, O God.
—Psalm 51:10

In a preceding verse David had prayed, *"Purge me with hyssop, and I shall be clean"* (Ps. 51:7). We said that a man becomes clean when he is sprinkled with the blood of Jesus and is cleansed and set free from his sin. In this verse David again prayed to be made clean, but this time the cleanness was to come in another way. He prayed that the Lord would *"create"* within him a clean heart. He wanted the Lord to make a new heart for him that was clean by His divine power.

David knew that there are two ways the unclean person can become clean before God. One is when he is washed and cleansed from his guilt in the blood of Jesus. He is judicially acquitted. The other happens when he is renewed, inwardly changed, and receives a new and clean heart in place of the old, unclean one. If you want to understand the way of salvation and the work of grace, strive to clearly understand this twofold purity.

Pronounced Not Guilty

First, you must understand how the soul becomes acquitted by the blood of Jesus. By the acquittal and forgiveness of God, a man is entirely freed from the guilt that is on him. Thus he is legally clean. That is to say, he has fulfilled the demands of the law, which requires that he pay for his guilt by himself or by another as his sacrifice. In that case, the law has nothing more to demand from him. He stands guiltless and clean. The law asks only about what he has done and what he has been. It does not ask what he still is or what he will do.

An earthly judge can acquit or pronounce clean without implying that the heart of the acquitted man is clean, or that he is beyond the possibility of committing the very same sin again. In like manner, the sinner is acquitted and pronounced clean from all the sins he has committed, without the implication that his heart is pure from the thought of future sins. Even though God knows the heart is inwardly impure as far as its sinful nature is concerned, the sinner is pronounced clean by the law as soon as all the demands of the law are fulfilled.

These demands have been fulfilled by the precious Savior's obedience and suffering. Therefore, the appropriation of Jesus' sacrifice has as its result the blessing of being pronounced clean in His blood. This is the purity David spoke of in the first half of the psalm. It is the complete forgiveness of sins, the being made *"whiter than snow"* (Ps. 51:7).

Cleansing the Heart

But this purity is not all the sinner needs. There is a second cleanness, the fruit and consequence of the first. An earthly judge can acquit a man or pronounce him clean even though his heart continues to hold on to his sins. He may leave the courtroom and commit them again. Yet God deals with us in a different manner. He acquits the sinner and pronounces him clean only for Jesus' sake. While He does not take into consideration the inward condition of the person's heart in terms of justification, He does not leave him that way.

As soon as He acquits him, He begins the work of inward purification. The very same grace that teaches the sinner to pray for the judicial cleansing by the acquittal of the law also teaches him to desire the second purity, the inward cleansing that comes through the renewing of the Spirit. Therefore, David, after he had prayed, *"Purge me..., and I shall be clean: wash me, and I shall be whiter than snow"* (v. 7), again prayed, *"Create in me* [inwardly] *a clean heart, O God."* The one is as necessary as the other. The two are one. They are merely two different ways by which the purity of Jesus comes to man. As soon as a person believes, the righteousness of Christ is totally his, and he is welcome to God as one who is clean. Yet the inward communication of the purity of Jesus to the soul takes place by degrees.

These two are one, but they should not be mixed together. Confusion over this point takes place too frequently, and souls are lost. The one cleanness is a root; the other is a fruit. The one goes first; the other follows after. Pay particular attention to this. David first prayed for the one. (See verses 7–9.) Then he asked for the other. Never forget that the first, the cleansing of the blood of Christ, is granted before you can inwardly receive the second. Only if you receive and accept the first will you have the power to obtain the second.

Let this be your prayer: *"Have mercy upon me, O God....Blot out my transgressions....Create in me a clean heart"* (Ps. 51:1, 10). Now we understand the place this prayer occupies in this psalm. It has better prepared us to feel its meaning and power. May God teach us to offer up this prayer earnestly and with our whole hearts.

Desire a Clean Heart

We must desire above all things to go on toward inward purity. David was not content praying merely for the forgiveness of his sins. No, he felt that his whole nature was inwardly corrupt. He also wanted to be inwardly purified. He simply would not be content with acquittal from punishment. Unfortunately, many are quite content with this. But David also wanted to be free from the power and indwelling of sin. He felt that only according to the measure of his holiness could he enjoy God. *"Blessed are the pure in heart: for they shall see God"* (Matt. 5:8). Let this be your desire.

This clean heart must also be your expectation. God the Creator is also God the Renewer. Just as the work of the first Creation was completed step-by-step, so also will it be with the renewal. The holy God can perform this work. He can make the unclean heart clean; it is not too hard for Him. This is what grace will do for you. Let your expectation reach for this blessing. When you pray for forgiveness, let it be a step toward becoming holy. God is pure and holy, and no prayer will be more welcomed by Him than that He make you holy also. *"Create in me a clean heart, O God."*

Chapter Eighteen

A Steadfast Spirit

And renew a right [steadfast] *spirit within me.*
—Psalm 51:10

When God creates a clean heart, then a person is born again. He is a new creature. He has received the new life, the love of God. Nevertheless, it is not enough for someone to receive the new life. He must grow and be strengthened. A weak child is a living human creature, but much has to be done for him in order to preserve, nourish, and lead that life until he becomes an adult. A weak child can stand and run, but he must also learn to stand fast. His behavior must also be established.

The Importance of Being Steadfast

This is what David prayed for next. He wanted not only a new life with a clean heart, but also a *"right* [steadfast] *spirit."* At the beginning, that new life and purity of heart are weak and tender. Much has to be done to make them grow. The Creation was not completed in one day. So it is also in the creation of a clean heart. Time is needed before everything is finished, and a person enters into his divine rest. After God has implanted the first principle of life in the new creation, that individual must willingly cooperate with God. He must with a *"right spirit"* surrender himself to the Lord and His work. The beginning of the new creation does not depend upon a steadfast spirit, but the progress of it does. The greater or less glory with which the creation will be brought to completion also depends on it.

Great loss may be brought about by separating these two prayers from one another. They are inwardly bound up with one another. The person who is simply satisfied that he has received a new heart does not persevere with a steadfast spirit to guard what he has received. If he does not try to use and increase what God has given him, the joy of the clean heart will become lost. On the other hand, the one who works faithfully and prays for this *"right spirit"* will have this purity of heart revealed within him. He will receive the full certainty and power of his heavenly birth.

We must also pray that God will give us a steadfast spirit. *Steadfast* is the opposite of weak, uncertain, changeable, variable. What stands fast cannot be moved or overthrown. Such a spirit must be asked from God in prayer. At the same time we must also observe in what ways God works and gives this blessing. This is the first thing that strikes us. Faith is a sure foundation. He who stands on it will not be moved. Therefore, we read in Psalm 112:8 of the righteous man, *"His heart is established, he shall not be afraid."* Peter wrote in 1 Peter 5:9 about being *"stedfast in the faith."* Paul also wrote in Colossians 1:22–23 that Christ has reconciled us and will present us *"holy and unblameable and unreproveable in his sight"* on the condition that we *"continue in the faith grounded and settled, and be not moved away from the hope of the gospel."*

Stand Fast on the Word of God

In Hebrew the word *believe* comes from a word that means "to be steadfast, to stand fast," and the word *believe* simply means "to continue steadfast." Since God is a steadfast Rock, the Foundation of all certainty and reliability, man becomes steadfast by faith in or by clinging to God.

The more you hold on to God and commit yourself to His Word and counsel, the more faithful you will stand. If you want to know how God will give you this steadfast spirit, it is by the Word. Let the Word of God be your food. Inwardly absorb and take hold of it. Let it penetrate you and be flesh and blood to your spirit.

Strive to think what God thinks and will what God wills. In everything be of the same mind that God is. Grow by His Word and have it dwell in you. Then you will be established. In all your wishes, expectations, desires, and efforts, let what God has said be your rule, and a firm spirit will be renewed in you. If the Word of God is the rock of your confidence, you will not be moved, just as there is *"no variableness, neither shadow of turning"* with God (James 1:17).

121

How did Abraham become strong in faith in the midst of so many severe trials? The root of his steadfastness was the promise of God. And why was it that Caleb and Joshua stood so firmly in the midst of the people of Israel? They held fast to the Word of God. And how did many other believers do the same? The answer is simple. *"They that trust in the LORD shall be as mount Zion, which cannot be removed, but abideth for ever"* (Ps. 125:1). The spirit obtains its steadfastness and strength from God in His Word.

A Steadfast Will

If you want to know how a steadfast spirit will manifest itself, the answer is not difficult. It will do so in the resoluteness of a steadfast will exercising dominion over the spirit and the walk. The great flaw in many believers who have a new heart is that they do not set themselves with a steadfast and resolute choice to cast out sin and do the will of God. They do not obey the orders of their conscience, the inward voice of the Spirit and the Word.

They do not surrender themselves to do the will of God as soon as they know it. There should be in every believer the holy purpose of doing the will of God without delay as soon as it is known. On this point I hope no uncertainty exists, for there are many double-hearted souls who are *"unstable in all* [their] *ways"* (James 1:8). Their divided hearts make them waver continually.

It is necessary to remember that, along with a new heart, a sense of sin, and good desire, there must also be a steadfast spirit that will be resolute. It must set itself positively to fulfill all the commands of God. This steadfast spirit must be a matter of much prayer: *"Renew a right* [steadfast] *spirit within me."*

At the same time, it must strengthen our battle against sin. He who seeks a *"right spirit"* in prayer will certainly receive it and be able to join in David's song of deliverance in Psalm 40:2: *"He brought me up also out of an horrible pit, out of the miry clay, and set my feet upon a rock, and established my goings."*

In the prayer for grace, in the life of grace, the steadfast spirit must have a place. The young tree must not only be planted, but also become deeply rooted; otherwise, it can bear no fruit. Therefore, let this be a continual prayer with you: "Make my footsteps steadfast in Your Word, and do not let any iniquity have dominion over me." Observe what the fruit of this prayer will be.

Chapter Nineteen

Living in God's Presence

Cast me not away from thy presence.
—Psalm 51:11

In his prayer, David proceeded to seek the blessings of the new life and also taught us by the Holy Spirit what we may expect from grace. The clean heart and the steadfast spirit are great blessings. But there is still something more that David desired—the light of God's countenance. He prayed for the blessed experience of always walking in the presence of God as His friend and knowing that God looked upon him with favor and love.

The Joy of God's Presence

The promise of this blessing in God's Word is very clear. It is frequently named as one of the privileges of God's children. For example, Psalm 89:15 says, *"Blessed is the people that know the joyful sound: they shall walk, O LORD, in the light of thy countenance."* It cannot be otherwise. What is the greatest joy of a child on earth? It is when his father or mother is pleased with him.

We often see that a little child plays quietly and contentedly when he is simply in a room with his mother. The mother is busy, and the child is busy, but just seeing his mother's face and knowing she is near brings joy to the child. God gives this privilege to those who receive from Him the name and the rights of children. In this world He always wants us to live before His face, in the light of His eyes, and with the assurance and experience of His love.

The value of this blessing is easily understood. What a heavenly joy it is to walk before the face of the Lord *"in the land of the living"* (Ps. 116:9). What a joy it is to do all our work and carry on our earthly endeavors at the feet of our Father, knowing that He looks down upon us with good pleasure. What a power it gives to be able to look up in every difficulty and in the middle of severe conflict and refresh ourselves with a glance at Him and be encouraged by His divine friendship. What a comfort it is in sorrow.

How can this blessing be enjoyed? The answer is not difficult. The child does not always need to be looking at his mother to enjoy being near her. The child is busy with his play or work, yet he immediately observes when his mother goes out. In the midst of all his work and play, he always has a hidden sense of her nearness. So it is with a true Christian. He can be so closely knit to his God that he cannot fail to sense His presence. In the midst of all his activities on earth, there always remains the blessed feeling that God sees him, and he can look up to Him.

He works under the eyes of God. Through this living and active faith, he beholds the Invisible One and abides in His light. Just as one walks and works in the light on earth without always thinking about it, so there flows around him the spiritual experience of the presence of God as the light of his soul.

We must understand what a vital part this experience plays in our spiritual lives. Do not forget that God's aim in His grace and your redemption is to restore the broken bond of fellowship and love between you and Him. True Christianity consists of the soul finding its highest happiness in personal communion with God.

Daily, unbroken fellowship between God and you is what grace gives. Every day you must try to walk in the light of God's presence. If you want to know how to get to the point of living so that you can enjoy this blessing, this psalm gives you the answer.

How to Live in God's Presence

In the first place, be aware of the forgiveness of your sins. Hold on to the grace that has blotted out your guilt. Every day bring each new sin to the blood of Jesus so that you can be washed from it again. Every day seek a living certainty of the grace that sees you in the righteousness of Jesus as being *"whiter than snow"* (Ps. 51:7). Look to the holy God who, for Jesus' sake, pronounced you righteous and loves you. Without this it will be impossible to walk in the light of God's presence. Remain secure in the faith that God is your God and your Father. Only by this faith can you continue in the enjoyment of the light and the love of God.

Second, strive earnestly to keep your heart pure and holy. Let the passion of your soul burn strongly against all inward impurity and sin. Guard against negative or unholy attitudes. Remember, you must hate sin as God hates it. Keep in mind that you are redeemed to be holy, as God is holy (1 Pet. 1:16). Let this be your fervent and earnest prayer: "A clean heart, O my God, a clean heart." Knowing that the work of the new creation is not finished at once, ask God to accomplish His work in you. A redeemed soul who remains content with what he has and does not earnestly desire to be holy cannot walk in the light of God's presence. His worldly thinking and his carnal attitudes are a cloud that separate him from God.

Third, maintain a steadfast spirit. You must have a solid determination of the heart, a firm choice of a strong will, to walk in God's presence. While you hold on to forgiveness and desire purity of heart, determine not to rest until you have experienced the blessing of always abiding in the pleasure of God's presence.

Begin every morning with this constant purpose, and seal it with believing prayer that God will keep you from everything that might turn you away from His presence. Let this be your will because it is also the will of God; then you will obtain the blessing. You will find that grace will do this for you. God will hear your prayer, *"Cast me not away from thy presence."* In this blessed experience you will be able to say with joy,

Oh how great is thy goodness,...u
thou hast wrought for them that tru
thee before the sons of men! Thou
hide them in the secret of thy pre.
from the pride of man: thou shalt
them secretly in a pavilion from the
of tongues. Blessed be the LORD: f
hath showed me his marvellous kin
in a strong city.　　　(Ps. 31:

Chapter Twenty

Asking for the Holy Spirit

Take not thy holy spirit from me.
—Psalm 51:11

D avid had sought a great blessing, a very gracious gift from God. He had asked that he might always walk before His presence and in the light of it. He had asked that his whole life be illumined by the immediate presence of God, living under His eye, and in His favor. David wanted his whole life on earth to be spent in communion with His God in heaven. Grace is prepared to give us this glorious life.

Walking on earth in fellowship with God in heaven is a wonderful experience. However, that the Most High would come down from His heaven *to dwell in my heart* and consecrate it to be His temple—certainly this is the full glory of what grace has destined for us. This is what David craved in the prayer, *"Take not thy holy spirit from me."* He yearned for the conscious indwelling of the Holy Spirit.

The First Work of the Spirit

Some may think that this petition is not in the proper place. Nothing is ever worked in us except by the Spirit. Even the first conviction of sin and the desire to pray for grace must come from Him. Should prayer for the Spirit, then, precede everything else? The answer to this question should be given several considerations.

The working of the Holy Spirit in a sinner who desires salvation is indeed essential, but it is a hidden and unconscious desire. The sinner does not know that the anxiety arising from the conviction of sin and his earnest pleas for mercy are the results of the Spirit's operations. On the other hand, when at a later time he does accept the Lord, he has the promise that he will know the Spirit. The Spirit will not only work in him, but will also establish His presence in him so that he will know and feel it.

This, for example, is the promise given to those who were baptized on the Day of Pentecost. They had already, at the outset, experienced the operation of the Spirit. *"Repent,...and ye shall receive the gift of the Holy Ghost"* (Acts 2:38). The Lord Himself said to His disciples after they had experienced the first workings of the Spirit, *"If ye love me, keep my commandments. And I will pray the Father, and he shall give you another Comforter"* (John 14:15–16).

The Believer's Pledge

David's prayer here is not a petition for the first operation of the Spirit with a view to conversion. Such prayer is necessary, and according to the will of God, it must be prayed. But the petition here in Psalm 51 asks for the indwelling of the Spirit of God that is the privilege of the believer. The Spirit dwells in us to teach us (see John 16:13–14), to seal us and to give us the assurance of sonship (see Romans 8:15–16), and to sanctify and prepare us for heaven. (See verse 11.)

This is the lesson taught to the believer in this petition. We can expect not only clean hearts, steadfast spirits, and the light of God's face, but also the indwelling of God's Spirit in our hearts. Every believer may have and ought to experience this blessing. Without this he does not live according to the will of God.

David's prayer makes this clear: *"Take not thy holy spirit from me."* He spoke as one who had already received the Holy Spirit. David asked that the Spirit not be taken from him. He felt that, although his former great sin had been forgiven, he still ran the risk of grieving and quenching the Holy Spirit. The Holy Spirit is the Spirit of grace who strives with sinners, but He is still the Holy Spirit who can be driven away by the love of sin.

David knew that our worldly ways, our fears, and our lack of attention to His workings can injure the Spirit. He is grieved, and He withdraws His presence from us. This also happens when we are unfaithful in the use of the means of grace, such as the Word and prayer, on which His work depends. It was with the sense of this great danger of grieving the Spirit that David prayed, *"Take not thy holy spirit from me."*

This petition is part of the prayer for grace. It is due to the grace of God only if the Holy Spirit is not taken away from believers. As often as injury is done to Him, He is dishonored and has reason to withdraw. Were He not the Spirit of grace, He would certainly leave us. David hoped and begged that the Spirit of God would not withdraw from him, even when he deserved to be left alone.

Lessons for the Believer

There are two lessons the believer can learn from David's prayer.

First, the Holy Spirit will dwell in the believer. If you desire to be led in the way of grace by the example of David—if you would see preserved and confirmed the blessings on which David's heart was set, namely, forgiveness, renewal, and restoration to the favor of God—you must keep yourself occupied with the promise of the Spirit. You must search in the Word of God for all the promises concerning the operation of the Spirit. You must know that this gift is presented to you. You must yield yourself completely to the Lord to experience this glorious grace. You must seek to live daily in the fellowship of the Spirit. You will discover that this is the highest blessing that can be experienced on earth.

In the second place, the blessing of the Holy Spirit must be a distinct request in the prayer for grace. The person who wants salvation must feel that he is unworthy of this blessing. Every day he must realize that God does him a favor by not taking away His Spirit. According to the sincerity of his desire, prayer, and faith, his growth in the

Holy Spirit will take place. His communion with the Spirit will become more conscious and effective. The neglect of David's prayer will result not only in the loss of this blessing, but also in the suppression of other blessings that have previously been enjoyed. Therefore, we should pray with all sincerity, *"Take not thy holy spirit from me."*

Chapter Twenty-One

The Joy of Salvation

Restore unto me the joy of thy salvation.
—Psalm 51:12

We have seen that David spoke of a twofold cleansing. First, there was a judicial cleansing that resulted in freedom from guilt. It is the fruit of the divine acquittal on the basis of the atonement of Christ, the being washed in the blood of Christ. Also, there was an inward cleansing worked out by the creative, renewing energy of the Holy Spirit.

David also spoke of a twofold joy, as we can see from the position of this request in the psalm. Previously he had said, *"Make me to hear joy and gladness"* (Ps. 51:8). This word stands between the repeated petition for forgiveness and relates this first joy to forgiveness of sins. The prayer that we have here in verse twelve teaches us that the joy of God's salvation is not only the desire and portion of those just converted. It is equally destined for the Christian who is striving on the pathway of growth and sanctification.

137

Joy and Forgiveness

Let us think carefully about this connection. We have already seen that the first joy of the person who has received salvation depends on the knowledge of forgiveness. The sinner becomes aware of his sin and cannot possibly rejoice in God unless he knows God as the One who has blotted out his sin. He knows that if he has not received this blessing, God is still his enemy and *"a consuming fire"* (Heb. 12:29). Only when the soul comes to the Cross and receives an interest in the atonement of Christ can the thought of the holy God fill him with gladness. It is fellowship with the reconciling God that brings joy.

In a similar manner, the continuance and growth of the soul's joy depends on deepening communion with God. The very first act of God, the forgiveness of sins, begins this fellowship with the soul and imparts gladness. God's next work in the soul is sanctification. Through His work of restoration, He establishes in it the clean heart and steadfast spirit, a life in the light of His presence, and the indwelling of the Holy Spirit. This also brings much joy.

Just as the soul cannot experience its first gladness without forgiveness, it cannot experience continued joy apart from a holy life. Just as the guilt of old sin robs the soul of joy until it knows it is forgiven, new sin that is not confessed fills the soul with darkness.

The joy of forgiveness will not always remain unless it is confirmed as the joy of sanctification. In this experience many Christians have had heavy losses, through lack of carefulness or knowledge. When the first joy begins to disappear, they do not know the cause or else they are unfaithful in not confessing the sad fact to God. They attribute the loss to God as a trial that He has sent to them.

If only they had asked for grace, not only to be washed from guilt but also to be liberated from the dominion of sin, they would have discovered that, with the progressive work of grace in the soul, a progressive joy would have been ministered to them by God. It is the joy of God's salvation for which David prayed. There is joy in God's salvation. As we yield ourselves to God for it, we will enjoy it.

So this twofold joy is one. We have already discussed this concept concerning the twofold purity. It is also true with the joy. It is sin that causes pain and misery. It is becoming free from sin that brings light and gladness. It is one God who rolls away the curse and guilt of sin in one moment, and then gradually makes the soul free from sin's power. The joy is also one.

Joy and Holiness

The person who rejoices in forgiveness ought to know that there is joy that is still sweeter, deeper, and more glorious than this. It takes place when the freedom from sin and fellowship with God are applied to living a holy life. The joy of forgiveness is the beginning for the newly born child of God. It is the milk of the blessing. The joy of sanctification and fellowship with God is for those who have grown up. It is the solid food, the ripe fruit of joy.

Let this petition sink deep into your heart. The joy and blessedness of God are His perfect holiness. The joy of His children is also the joy of holiness. Without a clean heart and a holy walk, the Christian cannot continuously experience joy.

The life of sanctification is joy. The way of a clean heart under the leading of the Spirit was once seen as a grievous way filled with groans and fears. God has changed it into a way of joy. At first, some sacrifice of the flesh may appear unwelcome and severe. But God has said that if you yield yourself to living a holy life, you will find in His service great reward and the joy of His salvation.

It is only as the salvation of God is actually experienced that joy can be tasted. Joy is not a separate gift that can be received and enjoyed apart from further experience of God's salvation. It is the joy of that salvation, and it is tasted as you surrender yourself to that salvation and the redeeming, sanctifying grace of God who gives it. There are so many Christians who seek the comfort and joy of redemption, and even pray for it, yet do not find it.

Others who are less anxious about joy and concentrate on seeing and tasting the salvation of God and doing all that He requires are glad in the Lord and filled with the joy of His salvation. If you want to be glad, simply cling to the Lord, the Source of all joy. If you want joy, surrender to the salvation of the Lord: first, in the assurance of forgiveness; second, in devotion to living a holy life. Then, with confidence, ask and expect a joy that is *"unspeakable and full of glory"* (1 Pet. 1:8).

Chapter Twenty-Two

Living in Freedom

Uphold me with thy free spirit.
—Psalm 51:12

Grace restores man to a right relationship with God. It also restores him to a right relationship to himself. As a result of this, he comes to have right attitudes toward his fellowmen. When grace makes the soul a partaker of the favor of God and the Spirit of God, the joy of God's salvation is poured out in the heart. As the fruit of this blessing, heart and mouth are opened to make others acquainted with the grace of God. It is this blessing that David next asked for from the divine mercy. He felt his calling, and he was aware of his weakness. In the midst of these feelings, he asked for help from above.

Being a Living Witness

David realized his calling. Every believer must be a witness and an example of the grace of God. He is obligated, for the honor of God and the salvation of others, to tell what great things the Lord has done for him. He knows that the living witness is better than dead legalism. Only when believers confess with boldness what God has done for them will the world be forced to acknowledge the work of God and adore His grace. Only by their speech and lifestyle can they prove that God is faithful.

In the world they must give convincing proof of what grace can really do. A candle is never lit among men to be hid under a bushel. (See Matthew 5:15.) The eternal God wants His people, *"the light of the world"* (v. 14), to let their lights shine (v. 16). David knew all this. Just as he confessed his sin and asked for redemption, he also prepared himself for the service of thanksgiving and of love.

David was also aware of his own weakness. The feeling that he expressed in Psalm 116:10, *"I believed, therefore have I spoken,"* was the expression of his own experience. He knew that unless he had the Spirit of faith, he could not know how to speak correctly. He realized that there was still in him the fear of man, as well as his own laziness and unfaithfulness. Therefore, it was important to him to pour out a prayer for this gift of divine grace, *"Uphold me with thy free spirit."*

Grace to Be a Witness

David knew he could count on the grace of God to give him this blessing. Grace is prepared to put the soul in a position to praise God and confess His name in the midst of every duty to which it is called. This is a point that believers do not understand. They feel that the forgiveness of sin is an act of mere grace on the part of God. They acknowledge that the sanctification of a life must also be worked out by grace. Yet they do not know that the *"free spirit,"* with its power, must also be the gift of free grace. They think that openly confessing the grace of God and proclaiming His goodness to others is the work they are expected to do for the Lord out of gratitude. But they do not feel adequate for this duty and remain helpless in their weakness and unfaithfulness, full of guilt and failure.

Some people are not aware that grace not only begins the work of redemption but also completes it. With the same certainty that they first prayed for forgiveness, they can also expect God to put them in a position to fulfill their vows of thanksgiving. It was with confidence that David prayed, *"Have mercy upon me....Uphold me with thy free spirit"* (Ps. 51:1, 12).

Freedom to Be a Witness

The words *"free spirit"* are very important. *"Where the Spirit of the Lord is, there is liberty"* (2 Cor. 3:17). There is freedom from all oppression, fear, and doubt that can weaken the soul. Only a complete surrender of the heart to be filled by the Spirit will bring freedom. It is only freedom before God that makes us free in our relationships with people. To have this full confidence before God, it is necessary that we look to Him, fellowship with Him, and be conscious of being surrendered to His will and service. The person who has this assurance in his heart before God never needs to fear any man. The continued awareness of God's friendship, nourished in fellowship with Him, will make us free from the dominion of the fear of man. It will also put us in a position to testify and praise God freely.

Believer, pray for a free spirit. Grace will certainly give it to you. You hinder the work of grace in your life if you remain without this blessing. You are content with half of what the grace of God is prepared to do for you. You defraud grace of the honor due to it if you remain satisfied without this gift. It is yours. It is your privilege to walk with a free spirit as a child of the heavenly King in the face of the world and sin.

Live the life of grace. Receive the blessings of redemption as they are presented in the verses of this psalm. Let the joy of God's salvation fill you. In answer to prayer, this free spirit will also become your most cherished possession. If you do not have it, let your faith stretch out and expect it. Pray with sincerity and earnestness: *"Uphold me with thy free spirit."* Out of the riches of the grace of God, you will certainly obtain it.

PART FIVE

THE SACRIFICE OF THANKSGIVING

*Then will I teach transgressors thy ways;
and sinners shall be converted unto thee.
Deliver me from bloodguiltiness, O God,
thou God of my salvation: and my tongue
shall sing aloud of thy righteousness. O
Lord, open thou my lips; and my mouth
shall show forth thy praise. For thou desirest not sacrifice; else would I give it:
thou delightest not in burnt offering. The
sacrifices of God are a broken spirit: a
broken and a contrite heart, O God, thou
wilt not despise. Do good in thy good
pleasure unto Zion: build thou the walls of
Jerusalem. Then shalt thou be pleased
with the sacrifices of righteousness, with
burnt offering and whole burnt offering:
then shall they offer bullocks upon thine
altar.*

—Psalm 51:13–19

Chapter Twenty-Three

Telling Others about Jesus

Then will I teach transgressors thy ways.
—Psalm 51:13

T he third part of this psalm begins here. The first part dealt with confession of sin. After this came prayer for the redemption David desired—forgiveness of sin and renewal of the heart by the Spirit of God. Now comes the fruit of redemption. He will praise the Lord and make His grace known to others. As a servant of God, he will submit himself to the great work of teaching sinners God's ways.

God's Purpose for You

For believers to share their faith with others is God's goal for every person to whom He makes His grace known. For all God's children this word holds true, *"This people have I formed for myself;*

they shall show forth my praise" (Isa. 43:21). This word agrees with the language of Paul,

> *Howbeit for this cause I obtained mercy,*
> *that in me first Jesus Christ might show*
> *forth all longsuffering, for a pattern to*
> *them which should hereafter believe on*
> *him to life everlasting.* (1 Tim. 1:16)

God must have honor from His work, and this honor is given to Him when a ransomed soul praises Him and speaks about the great things He has done for him.

Again, on earth no one lights a candle and puts it under a bushel. (See Matthew 5:15.) Neither would the Most High God of heaven do it. To everyone He brings out of the kingdom of darkness He says, *"Ye are the light of the world....Let your light... shine"* (vv. 14, 16). If you have offered up this prayer for grace to teach others, then fix your attention on what the Holy Spirit can teach you from David's prayer. The intention of grace is to make you a witness for the love of God and a monument of His wonderful goodness. Surrender yourself to this aim and plan of God. Say in His strength when you pray for grace, *"Then will I teach transgressors thy ways."*

Motivated by Love

God does not require this teaching as a debt you must pay in return for your redemption. If you will yield yourself to this work in the strength of grace, it will be your greatest joy to say, *"Then will I teach transgressors thy ways."* When you think of the pit out of which you have been rescued and the glorious salvation that is yours, your heart will be filled with compassion for sinners. When you think of the deep misery of others and how God's precious grace is ready to redeem them as it has redeemed you, you will consider it a blessing to exercise the privilege of speaking to them about Jesus.

When you think about what the love of Jesus has done for you, and how much you have to thank Him for, this love will motivate you. As often as you pray, "O God, have mercy on me. Then will I teach transgressors Your ways," the desire will be awakened in you for others to know Him as you know Him. You can be sure that only then will they be truly happy. Then they also will glorify the Lord. You feel, more than you can express in words, how worthy He is to be known and glorified.

The Joy of Telling Others

The thought that a sinner might be awakened to life, that a worldly person might be changed into an example of the grace of God— through your prayer and teaching—is enough to make your heart burst with joy. And this will not seem impossible if you look to Him to make use of your service.

You probably think you are unprepared for this task. You do not know how you will ever be in a position to teach sinners God's ways. The joy and gladness of redemption are almost taken away from you for fear of having to face this awesome duty. Observe that this promise results from a prayer for grace. David merely said that, if

God showed him favor, restored to him the joy of His salvation, and granted him the upholding of a free spirit, then he would *"teach transgressors [His] ways."* The Lord does not require more of you than what He Himself will enable you to perform.

To a person who has had his heart filled with grace, it is a joy and pleasure to make others acquainted with Jesus. The reason it is so difficult to speak about Jesus is that we are content with so little of the grace of God. We do not yield ourselves to be completely filled with it. Let the fear you feel convince you that you do not yet have as much grace as God is prepared to give. God will gladly give every soul so much blessing that his mouth will overflow because his heart is full. He will not be able to remain silent. Love for Jesus and for others will force him to speak.

Go to God more earnestly with prayer for the full joy of the forgiveness of sins and for the full indwelling of the Spirit. Then you also will teach transgressors His ways. This is what God desires from those who have been enriched with His grace. It is through this service that you will discover true joy and the full power of grace.

You ask where, when, to whom, and how you are to teach God's ways. The Lord will make all this known to you. The compulsion of love will teach you. Love will seek and create opportunities. Are you ill? You still have a great opportunity to teach others. Is your circle of friends narrow and limited? In your own house there may be someone who does not know God's ways. Are you simple and uneducated? The plain words of an ordinary person often find the fullest entrance into the hearts of others.

The world is full of transgressors, and the heart of Jesus is full of love. If you have really tasted His love, you must admit that the most glorious work is being the messenger of this love to redeem those who are going to hell. This grace that made you born again is also able to open your mouth to speak this wonderful blessing to others. Every person who has been given grace is called to the work of teaching sinners God's ways. You will receive strength to carry it out with a willing, joyful heart.

Chapter Twenty-Four

Being Used by God

And sinners shall be converted unto thee.
—Psalm 51:13

We have seen how deeply David felt about his sin. If there was anyone who had reason to be ashamed, never to trust himself, and to be silent, it was David. If there was anyone who had reason to say he did not know what might happen to him, it was David. If there was anyone who, because of his unfaithfulness, had reason to say that he had no right to speak; that no one was under an obligation to listen to him; that because of his sin, his words would have little impact, it was David. How exalted David had been in other days, but how deeply he had fallen!

In this psalm, David was in communion with God and His grace. In his prayer, he already anticipated the glory of God's grace. He felt that the grace of God was more powerful than his sin. Since grace could take away his sin before God, it could also give him access to men. He felt that if grace redeemed him, the chief of sinners, and showed its great goodness to him, it would also be prepared to make use of him as a blessing to others. Therefore, he not only promised, *"Then will I teach transgressors thy ways"* (Ps. 51:13), but he also believed that God would certainly bless his work: *"Sinners shall be converted unto thee."* He trusted in grace for others as he did for himself. The grace that had blessed him would make him a blessing. *"Then will I teach transgressors thy ways; and sinners shall be converted unto thee."*

There is power in the confidence that there will be blessing on our work. A person can work with enthusiasm and pleasure when he knows that God will give the increase. (See 1 Corinthians 3:7.) How can we cultivate this confidence? Let us carefully consider the source of our confidence.

Confidence in God

First of all, remember that conversion occurs when certain things are done. "I will teach transgressors; sinners will be converted." It is not enough to mourn over the poor, unbelieving world. It is not even enough to pray for the conversion of sinners. Something more is needed: *they must be taught.* This teaching should not be done just on the Sabbath or handed over to preachers of the Gospel. Every believer must within his own circle of friends faithfully perform and carry out the promise. After praying, *"Have mercy upon me"* (Ps. 51:1), the promise must follow, *"Then will I teach"* (v. 13). God is faithful to bring about conversion. What a marvelous change would take place in our churches if every believer would become a witness for God. Faithful witnessing would encourage the expectation that *"sinners shall be converted unto thee."*

Observe in what spirit we are to witness. David said that, as one who was pardoned and had received forgiveness from God and the joy of His salvation, he would teach transgressors. How many preachers, Sunday school teachers, Christian elders, and friends there are whose teaching has no power! They never see the fulfillment of the hope: *"Sinners shall be converted unto thee."* It is not from lack of teaching the truth, but from failing to speak about a living experience of this grace. They teach from a knowledge of the truths of Scripture or refer to an earlier spiritual experience. But this is not enough. If you want to see teaching and conversion of sinners, you must have a living, effective experience of the grace of God. Blotting out your guilt in a daily use of the blood of Jesus must be the joy of your soul.

Your Christian walk must be carried out by purifying your heart and renewing a steadfast spirit in your inner being. With the prayer, *"Take not thy holy spirit from me"* (Ps. 51:11), your whole being must be one where Jesus lives in your heart. With the sincere petition, *"Uphold me with thy free spirit"* (v. 12), this purpose must be renewed continually and acted on: *"Then will I teach transgressors thy ways"* (v. 13).

This must be your effort and your prayer. When you say with the desire of this psalm, *"Then will I teach,"* you may also add, *"Sinners shall be converted unto thee."* Let your teaching of others be the fruit of His indwelling grace. Then it cannot remain unblessed. Wash daily in the blood of Jesus, and seek the anointing of His Spirit. Live near to Jesus, and *"sinners shall be converted."*

Confidence in Prayer

Observe that this confidence must be nourished and expressed in prayer. David did not look to himself and his own power. It was while he looked to God in prayer that David spoke these glorious words of faith. Speak this prayer on your knees, with your eyes fixed on God who has shown you His grace. This hope is not too much to expect—"I will teach, and sinners will be converted." If at the beginning you do not succeed in using these words in full faith, then pray the prayer again. Express the hope again to Him who sits on the throne of grace.

Begin with the starting point, *"Have mercy upon me, O God"* (Ps. 51:1), and climb this ladder of prayer by the various steps of the spiritual life. Make sure of each stage in your own heart until you come to this: *"Then will I teach transgressors"* (v. 13). The Spirit of prayer, who has taught you to use all the other petitions, will enable you to speak this word with increasing confidence, *"Sinners shall be converted unto thee."* Just as prayer and conflict became the power that led you to speak this word, so will this word become your power to say to sinners, "Sinners shall be converted; I will teach transgressors."

"Have mercy upon me, O God....Then will I teach transgressors thy ways; and sinners shall be converted unto thee" (vv. 1, 13).

Chapter Twenty-Five

Delivered from Guilt

Deliver me from bloodguiltiness, O God,
thou God of my salvation.
—Psalm 51:14

D avid had made a great promise. He was to teach transgressors God's ways. At the same time, he had expressed his expectation that by his teaching, sinners would be converted. The words were scarcely out of his lips when he again felt how sinful he was, and how it could only be through supernatural grace that such a result would ever be achieved. He felt that Uriah's blood had defiled him in the presence of God and man. If God would give him the perfect, living assurance that he was fully acquitted from his sins, then he would be able to praise God in truth.

A Daily Reality

A living, personal experience of grace is necessary if we are to tell others about Jesus. No one can waver in the enjoyment of his own redemption. The memory of forgiveness and grace experienced at an earlier stage is not enough. Every day there must be a renewal of the divine assurance that we are redeemed by God. There must be a living reality of salvation as a present fact, a continually renewed and fresh exercise of fellowship with the God of redemption. The person who does not know God in this way cannot make Him known to others. David felt this. How could he, the murderer of Uriah, stained with the guilt of blood, bring life to others while he must still give an account of the blood of Uriah?

It is impossible for me to teach others if I do not know God correctly myself. And man does not truly know God if he does not know Him as the God of forgiveness. Moreover, this knowledge cannot be living and real if it is not continually renewed from heaven by the Holy Spirit. Every time I give my testimony to teach sinners so that they will be converted, it must be with the prayer, *"Deliver me..., O God, thou God of my salvation: and my tongue shall sing aloud of thy righteousness"* (Ps. 51:14).

The Guilt of Sin

When one considers the words of this petition closely, these thoughts will be more fully confirmed. Let us think about the word that is used here in this prayer: *"**Deliver** me from bloodguiltiness."* This concept of deliverance is one that we have not previously seen in this psalm. It is commonly used, not so much of setting free from sin, as of deliverance from enemies who pursue and oppress us. An example of this usage is the prayer, *"Deliver us from evil"* (Matt. 6:13). It is from this point of view that David here contemplated his sins.

David believed that God had forgiven him, and he was also assured that he had been cleansed from his sins. Yet sometimes there are occasions in a believer's life when sins that have been forgiven rise up again and pursue and overtake the soul. God has forgiven them, but the person who committed them cannot forget them. He is afraid there will be a new outbreak of their evil. The great enemy, Satan, makes use of these times of oppression to utterly cast our souls down to the dust. In that case there is only one remedy. God alone can deliver us from the heavy burden of guilt.

But He can do it. He can give us such a view of the completeness of His forgiveness and grace that we will be delivered out of the hands of our enemies and know that sin will have no more dominion over us. He can make us understand the full significance of the glorious words of the New Testament, *"He was manifested to take away our sins"* (1 John 3:5), in order that we may have *"no more conscience of sins"* (Heb. 10:2). Through the Holy Spirit, God fully reveals to us the redemption of the Lord Jesus, so that we have the full answer to the petition, *"Deliver me from bloodguiltiness, O God, thou God of my salvation."*

The enjoyment of such complete deliverance becomes the urgent desire to sing of His righteousness. If you do not know if you can celebrate God's praise, come and experience this blessing.

Let it become a matter of living knowledge in your heart how glorious it is to be delivered by God. Then your mouth will sing the praises of God.

Personal Salvation

This same idea is found in the very name by which David designated God: *"O God, thou God of my salvation."* It is because he is the God of my salvation that I joyfully want to praise Him. The personal relationship between God and men and the living assurance and experience of it are essential for this to take place. At the same time, this experience empowers me to make Him known. If you want to know how to succeed in calling God by this name, learn from David's example.

In the beginning of this psalm, David was not prepared to use the possessive term. Several times, he addressed the Lord as "God," but not as "my God." Under the power of continued prayer, as well as the constantly renewed plea for grace, his faith was strengthened. The Spirit of God had given him courage to hold fast to God. *"Thou art the God of my salvation"* (Ps. 25:5).

It is the same with you. If with every sin, old or new, you cast yourself before Him, pleading for the fullness of His grace—forgiveness, renewal, and complete redemption—you will be given courage in the midst of such prayer to say with all the spiritual freedom of faith, *"God of my salvation."* May all who are looking for this assurance of faith come to a full understanding of it. It is not a matter for argument, but it is learned in prayer. The one who wants to truly say to Him,

"You are my God, the God of my salvation," must obtain the privilege in prayer.

When a person has learned to use this language of faith toward God, it will not be so difficult to use it toward men. It is impossible to speak freely with God and yet hesitate to speak with people. As we speak to God in secret, we must confess Him in public. The principal characteristic of the proclamation of the Good News to others is the confession, "He is the God of *my* salvation. What He has done for me, He can also do for you. I speak from experience. What the Word says, I confirm with all the certainty of personal knowledge. The God who has redeemed me will also redeem you."

Chapter Twenty-Six

The Meaning of Righteousness

My tongue shall sing aloud of thy righteousness.
—Psalm 51:14

After the petition comes the promise. Grace does not selfishly desire personal enjoyment or safety, but gives itself to honor God and bless others. David's experience of fellowship with God, as the God of his salvation, caused him to praise God. *"Deliver me from bloodguiltiness, O God, thou God of my salvation: and my tongue shall sing aloud of thy righteousness"* (Ps. 51:14).

The words of this promise are very significant and instructive. First of all, observe the main theme of this joyful celebration. It is the *"righteousness"* of God. It is as if this psalm of grace and redemption could not end without this word in which the work of God in connection with our redemption is presented. The Holy Spirit uses the righteousness of God to indicate to us the origin, way, and fruit of our redemption.

The Righteousness of God

Righteousness embraces in one word an attribute of God, the gift with which we are endued, and the operation of this redemption in our lives. For the person who wants to be saved or for those who have been recently converted, the word *grace* has a beautiful sound and appears to be most attractive and encouraging. Yet the growing knowledge of grace will always bring us to the righteousness of God, where the love of God has its foundation and in which the believer seeks his stability. Therefore, to the first promise to teach transgressors God's ways, these thought is added: the resolve to proclaim His righteousness. Let us try to understand this word.

First of all, *righteousness* indicates the attribute of God that moves and guides Him in the giving of grace. Grace in the forgiveness of our unrighteousness is not exhibited at the expense of the righteousness of God. *"Grace reign*[s] *through righteousness"* (Rom. 5:21). It is from the righteousness of God that grace receives its power. So John wrote, *"If we confess our sins, he is faithful and just* [or righteous] *to forgive us our sins"* (1 John 1:9). Paul said that God is righteous when He justifies the ungodly. (See Romans 3:26; 4:5.) In the Psalms and the Prophets, this righteousness of God is frequently mentioned as that which His people especially celebrate and rejoice.

Some people have not been able to understand this concept; they think that in these passages the word *righteousness* must be the same thing as *goodness*. This is not the case. The righteousness of God, His character that always does what is right, is the foundation of His throne of grace. Believers understand that the only way the unrighteous can be redeemed and become righteous is that God, the only Righteous One, will communicate His righteousness to them.

The Righteousness of Christ

The phrase *"thy righteousness"* further means the righteousness that is given to the sinner in God's gracious sentence of acquittal. David prayed, *"Wash me, and I shall be whiter than snow"* (Ps. 51:7). That condition of being *"whiter than snow"* can be maintained only in the possession of the righteousness of God. The New Testament makes it plain how this can be. The righteousness of God is brought to us by the Mediator, the Man Christ Jesus. By His obedience and suffering, Jesus has brought us an everlasting righteousness.

Just as by the sin of the First Adam death reigned over all who belong to him, so through the righteousness of the Second Adam grace comes to all who cling to Him. (See Romans 5:12, 15, 17.) As *"faith was reckoned to Abraham for righteousness"* (Rom. 4:9), so through all succeeding periods of Israel's history, it is the grace of God that justifies the ungodly and has been the hope and joy of His people. *"In the LORD shall all the seed of Israel be justified, and shall glory"* (Isa. 45:25).

The Joy of Righteousness

This word also signifies the effect of the grace of God. The sentence of acquittal by which God justifies the sinner and the righteousness of

Christ that the sinner obtains become power for sanctification. They are in him the seed of a new life of righteousness. *"He that doeth righteousness is righteous, even as he is righteous"* (1 John 3:7). *"Grace reign[s] through righteousness unto eternal life"* (Rom. 5:21). Grace renews the soul after the likeness and spirit of the Righteous One. The righteousness of God in Christ, first assigned by faith, becomes the new nature in which God's children walk. *"If ye know that he is righteous, ye know that every one that doeth righteousness is born of him"* (1 John 2:29).

According to the New Testament the full significance of the concept of the righteousness of God in this psalm is that we receive His righteousness. And it was in regard to this truth that David said, *"My tongue shall sing aloud of thy righteousness."* The revelation of it was so delightful and worthy of admiration that David wanted not only to speak of it, but also to celebrate its value and worth. He gloried in it as something that had now become his. Joyfully he praised God for it. This was not a burden on him or a mere fulfillment of duty; it was something that was his delight. He spoke of it with joy and gladness.

On every occasion, draw near to God for a new experience of the righteous grace of the Lord in complete deliverance from your guilt. Then you will joyfully celebrate the righteousness of the Lord. Every repetition of the prayer, *"Deliver me..., O God, thou God of my salvation"* (Ps. 51:14), will give you strength and joy for the promise, *"And my tongue shall sing aloud of thy righteousness."*

Chapter Twenty-Seven

Speaking Forth
His Praises

*O Lord, open thou my lips; and my mouth
shall show forth thy praise.*
—Psalm 51:15

The promise to praise God is repeated again. It is preceded, however, by the prayer that grace will give the strength to fulfill it. We have already seen that the full, living experience of God's salvation will agree to praise God. On the other hand, this worship without the experience is an impossibility. Furthermore, it is a gift asked in prayer and then obtained.

Excuses for Silence

This petition reminds us of the natural reluctance and inability of man to speak of God and to witness of His grace. Every believer's experience confirms this truth. We keep silent even

167

when we enjoy the grace of God and eagerly desire to work for Him. Sometimes it is our fear of mockery and contempt from others. At other times it is unbelief or a feeling of being unprepared that takes away all courage and delight in witnessing. There is also that hidden self-centeredness that finds an excuse in its own spiritual need. Another excuse is humility that is afraid of injuring God's name by confessing Him now and later becoming disloyal and unfaithful. Many believers could tell of a time when they wanted to work for the Lord. They could tell of the months and years they spent wishing and longing until their silence became a habit and their consciences, by all sorts of excuses, became passive.

If only they had understood what the difference is between sinful silence and impetuous speech. If only they had understood that, along with the forgiveness of sins and the renewal of the life, grace will also give the ability to speak. The continued prayer, "Have mercy on me, O God; open my lips," will be heard.

The Lord Helps Us Speak

This prayer recorded here by the Spirit of God assures us that the Lord can and will open the lips. The one who sincerely desires to believe this truth simply has to reflect on what is recorded in the Word of God. Read the history of Moses. Let the wonderful arguments by which God showed him His power to give him a speaking mouth sink deep into your soul. (See Exodus 4:10–12.) Everyone who will humbly listen to these divine words of encouragement will be strengthened in this confidence.

Also, read the stories of the calling of Jeremiah (see Jeremiah 1:7–9) and the other prophets. See how fully God presents the power to speak as one of His gifts. Consider the promises of the Old Testament about the gift of the Spirit and observe how it is accompanied by the power to speak. Notice the predictions of Jesus concerning witnessing for Him as the fruit of the gift of the Spirit. (See John 15:26–27; Acts 1:8.) Remember that on the Day of Pentecost the first manifestation of the power of the exalted Christ was the filling of the mouths of the disciples with God's praise.

A high calling and divine certainty are attached to the opening of the lips as a gift of grace. It truly belongs to us. *God can give it.* He has done it for thousands. *God will give it.* It is necessary for the accomplishment of His glorious work of grace. *God shall give it.* His promises are faithful. "Lord, open my lips." We have as much right to this prayer as to the other, *"Have mercy upon me, O God"* (Ps. 51:1). The one is heard as certainly as the other.

The Gift of Speaking

David's prayer teaches us the way to obtain this gift. Whenever we mention a speaking mouth, one thinks of natural gifts. If he does not, then he imagines that what has been said does not apply to him. He will try to serve God in other ways. He will thank God with his money, influence, and example. This is good, but it will not free anyone from the obligation of fulfilling his calling to bring to God the sacrifice of the lips. One of the tokens of the coming of the kingdom of God was that not only would the blind see, but also the mute would speak and praise God.

The grace of God does not take the darkness from the eyes just so that the soul can know Him. It also opens the mouth to praise Him. Not only is an unclean spirit cast out, but also the demon that was mute. Along with the Holy Spirit, all the disciples were given mouths to praise God. In heaven there are no mute men and women. Every tongue praises God. The Christian whose tongue is not loosened or liberated is defective. He is lacking one of the most glorious capabilities of the new man.

It is not a question of whether you have a natural gift for speaking. Many people who speak briefly and weakly receive from grace the capacity for achieving great results with their small gift. It is not the beauty of the language. It is the power of the life and spirit that the blessing depends on. Let your desire to receive this grace become stronger, under a sense of your solemn obligation to praise God and make Him known. Let every experience of weakness and inability urge you to find confidence in the power and promise of God. Out of such desire and confidence let the prayer rise, *"Lord, open thou my lips; and my mouth shall show forth thy praise."* The answer will not be far off. This decision may cause you much conflict and perseverance. This rich petition is not learned in one day. The riches of grace are not exhausted in one day. Yet if you have the desire, you will obtain the blessing. Therefore, every time we use the prayer, *"Have mercy upon me, O God"* (Ps. 51:1), let us also add the petition, *"Lord, open thou my lips; and my mouth shall show forth thy praise."*

Chapter Twenty-Eight

The Sacrifice of Love

For thou desirest not sacrifice; else would I give it:
thou delightest not in burnt offering.
—Psalm 51:16

D avid had surrendered himself to God in the joy of deliverance and thanksgiving. From then on, he would live to honor and praise God. Nevertheless, he felt how little he could do. The question arose within him, Is there not something more the Lord desires from me? He thought of sacrifices. By multiplying these, could he not accomplish a work that would be acceptable to the Lord? As soon as the question arose, it became clear that God does not delight or have pleasure in sacrifices.

The clearness with which David felt and expressed this truth is one of the deep spiritual lessons of this psalm. In the hidden part, God had made him to know wisdom (Ps. 51:6). He was more aware of his sin than ever before. He knew grace in its high spiritual power. He had experienced the wonderful work of God in forgiveness and renewal. He had learned to understand the symbolic sprinkling and washings recorded in the Old Testament. He had experienced how God washes and purifies the soul. Now the Spirit had also unfolded to him the life of thankfulness and shown him how insufficient external sacrifices would be.

Two Kinds of Sacrifices

Under the old covenant there were two kinds of sacrifices: sin offerings and guilt offerings for atonement, and thank offerings and burnt offerings to represent dedication to God. Discovering the depths of sin caused David to feel the need of something more than an external atonement. Now he understood that it was an inward, spiritual dedication that God wanted from him.

In all these respects, this psalm is a prophecy of the grace of the New Testament. It is in this statement, *"Thou desirest not sacrifice,"* that the difference between the Old and New Testament lies. Under the old covenant and according to the law, man must always bring to and give to God something for taking away sin. In the Gospel, on the other hand, God brings to man and gives to him what can atone for sin. Under the old covenant, man must bring sacrifice to God in the hope that He will receive it. Under the new covenant, God comes to man with a Sacrifice, in order that he may receive it and be blessed.

This is the meaning of the word of the prophet repeated by Jesus when He said to the Pharisees, *"But go ye and learn what that meaneth, I will* have mercy, and not sacrifice" (Matt. 9:13). To require and bring sacrifices was the characteristic of the old covenant, but to show and receive mercy is the glory of the new covenant. So the one who would fully enjoy the salvation of the Gospel must, above all, try to understand the words, *"Thou desirest not sacrifice."*

Mercy, Not Sacrifice

This word reminds us of the freedom of God's grace as a source of blessing. The spirit of the law—trying to earn righteousness through the works of the law—is so natural to us that we are inclined to see God as a hard, austere man (see Matthew 25:24; Luke 19:21–22) who makes heavy demands on us. If only we could abandon this attitude. God is a God who does not demand but gives freely. The secret of fellowship with Him is always to look to Him as a God from whom one may ask and expect everything. He delights in mercy and not in sacrifice.

This is true of the first grace of forgiveness. How long did you think that there was something you had to do in order to receive God's grace? How long did you think there was something you had to bring and offer in order to be acceptable to God? When faith became plain to you as simply receiving what God had done for you and offered to you, your response was, "Is that all? Is salvation so near and so easy to find?" Then you learned what is meant by saying, *"Thou desirest not sacrifice."*

The same thing is also true of the higher grace of sanctification. Holiness is not something we must accomplish. Holiness is only in God. We become holy only as He makes us share in His holiness. Christ has been given to us for justification and sanctification. The one who understands this truth enjoys the salvation of the life of grace as a continuous reception of the fullness of Christ. He knows he no longer has to represent the life of divine salvation as a severe sacrifice, but as a glorious experience of what the grace of God works in him. Obedience is something higher than sacrifice. This deeply significant statement reveals the secret of the true service of God. It is not what man does or brings to God, but the childlike attitude of loving submission that is the true fulfillment of the law.

The believer who thought of service to God primarily as difficult and requiring self-sacrifice can now discover the joy of the life prepared for him through the compassion of God in Christ. His service to God becomes a service in the joy of love. Love does not speak of sacrifices. Others may glory in the sacrifices that love brings, but love does not consider them to be sacrifices. They are a joy and a delight.

When we become aware of the gracious attitude of God toward us, we can apply this word to our relationships with other people, *"I will have mercy, and not sacrifice"* (Matt. 9:13). We can meet the unsaved with compassion and tenderness, not with the hard requirements of the law. We can understand the secret of the love by which transgressors learn God's ways, and by which sinners are converted to Him. *"Thou desirest not sacrifice"* is the gospel of personal comfort that can be joyfully proclaimed to others.

Chapter Twenty-Nine

Maintaining a Broken Spirit

The sacrifices of God are a broken spirit:
a broken and a contrite heart, O God,
thou wilt not despise.
—Psalm 51:17

I n the beginning of the psalm, David had, out of his deep guilt, revealed that his heart was broken. We have seen that a contrite spirit is a definite characteristic of the person seeking grace. In the course of the psalm, however, David's tone underwent a change. He had spoken of *"joy and gladness"* (Ps. 51:8) and had given promises full of courage and strength. You might think that a broken heart is necessary at first, but later on, when grace has done its work, this broken condition is no longer important. As a matter of fact, it is quite the contrary. Even in the life of grace, from the beginning to the end, God is especially pleased with the attitude of *"a broken and a contrite heart."* This is an abiding and unmistakable feature of the life of thanksgiving that the Spirit wants us to experience. *"The sacrifices of God are a broken spirit."*

The Broken Spirit

This statement teaches us how the broken spirit will, for the believer, always be a token of grace. God, according to His promise, forgets sin, but the believer never forgets it. Being a sinner is not something superficial and temporary. To maintain and enjoy the right kind of fellowship with the Lord, we must always be mindful of who we are and how much we are indebted to His grace. It is just as the Lord said to redeemed Israel:

> *And I will establish my covenant with thee; and thou shalt know that I am the LORD: that thou mayest remember, and be confounded, and never open thy mouth any more because of thy shame, when I am pacified toward thee for all that thou hast done, saith the Lord GOD.*
>
> (Ezek. 16:62–63)

It is not just the sense of guilt, but the power of grace and forgiving love that melts, humbles, and bruises the soul before God. Often, it is just the glorious proof of the goodness of God that overwhelms the soul and makes it remain contrite in the awareness of its own unworthiness.

God has no delight in sacrifice and no pleasure in the greatest external offerings that may be brought to Him. His sacrifice is *"a broken spirit."* It is at the inner man, the hidden man of the heart, that He looks. It is in spirit and truth that He wants to be worshipped. (See John 4:23–24.) The sacrifice that He desires is a living, spiritual sacrifice. If we feel we have very little to bring to the Lord, this word comes with grateful comfort: *"A broken and a contrite heart, O God, thou wilt not despise."* This verse reminds us that the Lord never delights in anything as much as that feeling of emptiness and failure that breaks the soul. This feeling makes the heart capable of receiving and appreciating the wonderful grace of God. This feeling teaches us to look away from ourselves and to seek everything in God. This contrite attitude gives glory to God alone. God bends over such a heart with inexpressible tenderness to gloriously fulfill the promises of His Word.

The Contrite Heart

Read the great statements of Isaiah on this point:

For thus saith the high and lofty One that inhabiteth eternity, whose name is Holy; I dwell in the high and holy place, with him also that is of a contrite and humble spirit, to revive the spirit of the humble, and to revive the heart of the contrite ones. (Isa. 57:15)

Thus saith the LORD, The heaven is my throne, and the earth is my footstool: where is the house that ye build unto me?

> *and where is the place of my rest? For all those things hath mine hand made, and all those things have been, saith the* LORD: *but to this man will I look, even to him that is poor and of a contrite spirit, and trembleth at my word.* (Isa. 66:1–2)

There is no place in the world in which the holy God, when He stoops from His glory, will so readily set up His throne as in the *"contrite spirit."* He also devotes much work to the accomplishment of this bruising of the heart in His children. By the sense of guilt, the experience of sin, through many trials, and the work of the Spirit, God prepares His own for bringing to Him the sacrifice that pleases Him most—a contrite heart.

Psalm 51:17 further teaches us to understand how the freedom and joy of the life of grace will be manifested in the broken heart and the contrite spirit. This thought seems to be a contradiction. Yet God's thoughts are not as our thoughts (Isa. 55:8). The more we practice His Word, the more we will experience how our need and God's grace are bonded to one another. His life can then be fully revealed in our death. We will see His power in our weakness, His comfort in our sorrow, His help in our inadequacy, His healing in our oppression, and His love in our brokenness. We will also experience that the more we die to ourselves and yield ourselves to the discipline of the Spirit, the more God's good pleasure and His nearness to the broken in heart will become ours.

When you lift up the petition, *"Have mercy upon me, O God"* (Ps. 51:1), do not forget that this verse concerning brokenness is closely connected with it. It is a word of anxiety but also a word of comfort. The value of this truth is felt in the confession of sin, the striving for holiness, the self-dedication of thanksgiving to praise God. *"The sacrifices of God are a broken spirit."* There is nothing in your Christian life that will enable you to find grace and to have influence with God and man alike as the holy ornament of a contrite spirit, which is of great price in the sight of God. *"A broken and a contrite heart, O God, thou wilt not despise."*

Chapter Thirty

Praying for Others

Do good in thy good pleasure unto Zion:
build thou the walls of Jerusalem.
—Psalm 51:18

David began this psalm with prayer for grace for himself. However, he could not end it with this same prayer. The blessed experience of grace made him think not only of unbelievers, but also of the people of God who would partake of this grace with him. For these he poured out his heart. He could never forget the people of God. This petitioning on behalf of others is an essential element of true prayer and a principal characteristic of the true believer. The true believer is also an intercessor. We should pay attention to the important lesson this verse teaches us.

Learning to Pray

In the first place, true intercessors for the church of God are those who have first learned to pray for themselves. Personal need is the school in which true intercessors are trained. It is in the confession of personal sins that the secret of believing intercession is learned. There are many in church and prayer meetings who pray for themselves and others, yet they know little of personal communication with God in the prayer, *"Cleanse me from my sin"* (Ps. 51:2).

First of all, the sinner must feel as if he has God's undivided attention. He must learn to deal with God for himself alone. Then he will learn to understand the grace of God and know how to plead for this blessing on behalf of the people and the city of the Lord. Then he not only obtains courage to speak of God to his fellowmen, but he also delights in doing so. He also feels he has power to speak and plead with God on behalf of his fellowmen.

Those who have learned to pray for themselves become intercessors of their own accord. Grace is not self-seeking. The love of God shed abroad in the heart creates love in God's people and church. (See Romans 5:5.) This was true of the nation of Israel. Think, for example, of the prayers of Ezra, Nehemiah, and Daniel (see Ezra 9; Nehemiah 9; Daniel 9), or the way the converted Saul of Tarsus continually prayed for the early churches. Intercessors such as these are called watchmen on the walls of Jerusalem. (See Isaiah 62:6–7.)

God makes us to be fellow workers with Him, and He is prepared to listen to us. At our urgent request, He will answer. As soon as there are several in a church who, in their own experience, learn to understand the grace of God exhibited in this psalm, the prayer meeting will include the petition, *"Do good...unto Zion."*

Appealing to God's Compassion

It is not just the experience of deliverance from personal sin that motivates people to pray. There is something more. David felt himself to be one with the people. He was afraid his sin might possibly prove harmful to the city as a whole, so he prayed that any serious consequences might be averted. Aware of the terrible power of sin to destroy, the intercessor asked the Lord to turn aside the dreaded evil and to do good to Zion according to His good pleasure.

"Do good in thy good pleasure unto Zion." It is to God's good pleasure in Zion that intercessors appeal when they ask Him to do good to her. The psalmist appealed to God's lovingkindness and the greatness of His compassion for His people. David's knowledge of God's character gave him power and courage to pray. We should never forget this. Our strongest argument in prayer is the being and heart of God. The more we cling to what God has revealed concerning His feelings toward His people and His purposes and promises, the more we will feel the power to pray. The good pleasure of God toward Zion is the foundation for our hope, the measure of our expectations, and the strength of our faith. If our souls were more fully possessed by this conviction, we would pray more earnestly, *"Do good...unto Zion."*

This great, overwhelming good will is expressed in the words, *"Build thou the walls of Jerusalem."* That petition includes *building up* where they were not yet completed, *rebuilding* where they were broken down by hostile attacks, and *outbuilding* where they had become too narrow for the growing number of inhabitants. It includes prayer for the new spiritual growth of the congregation, for the maintenance of God's authority, and for the extension of the kingdom of God by the ingathering of those who do not yet know Him. The believer who has tried to understand God's plan for the heavenly city will certainly feel how necessary this prayer is in our time. Zion, the City of God, the dwelling place of the Most High, will exhibit the splendor of the New Jerusalem. (See Revelation 21:10–11.) In the midst of severe toil and conflict, disappointment and hindrances, living stones are being laid, and the walls slowly rise. (See 1 Peter 2:5.)

"Build thou the walls of Jerusalem." Believers need to make this their prayer because of their unbelief and worldliness. In view of the needs of millions who do not know the Lord, let the grace shown to you cause you to pray, *"Do good in thy good pleasure unto Zion: build thou the walls of Jerusalem."*

Chapter Thirty-One

Pleasing God with Our Sacrifices

Then shalt thou be pleased with the sacrifices
of righteousness, with burnt offering
and whole burnt offering: then shall they
offer bullocks upon thine altar.
—Psalm 51:19

When God in His good pleasure will do good to Zion and build the walls of Jerusalem, a glorious time will dawn for the people of God. Then, according to David, God will be pleased with the sacrifices brought to Him. The people also will have delight and offer these sacrifices with gladness upon the altar. In an earlier verse David had said, *"Thou desirest not sacrifice"* (Ps. 51:16). Those words show the deep spiritual insight David had concerning the inferiority of the old covenant sacrifices. God could not desire these offerings because they were the work of man. God desired something higher and better in the all-sufficient sacrifice of

His Son. (See Hebrews 10:5–10.) David now understood that when Zion was again visited by God, He would again be pleased with the sacrifices of righteousness.

Our Relationship to God

We are taught very important lessons in this verse. First of all, we see how the worth of our religion depends entirely on our relationship to God. The very same psalm that says, *"Thou desirest not sacrifice"* (Ps. 51:16), says later, *"Then shalt thou be pleased with the sacrifices of righteousness."* In the interval between these two statements, a great change has taken place. Since sin has been atoned for, the good pleasure of God must now rest upon Zion. Her sacrifices must be acceptable to Him.

The sacrifices are no longer brought to take away unrighteousness, but they are a symbol of the dedication and thanksgiving of a justified people. They are sacrifices that God can really take pleasure in. This truth teaches us something about our fellowship with God. The value of all our works is defined by our relationship to God. If we are not reconciled to God and have not received atonement and forgiveness of sins in Christ, then our best works cannot be pleasing to God. If, on the other hand, we have become the children of God and the relationship between Him and us is as it should be, then He takes delight in our service and works. They are acceptable to Him. It is said, in the words of David, *"Thou desirest not sacrifice"*; but he also said, *"Then shalt thou be pleased with the sacrifices."*

The same is true in the words of Paul. First we read, *"Not of works"* (Eph. 2:9); but he also wrote, *"Created...unto good works"* (v. 10). The very same works that, before faith, are deserving of rejection are, after faith, an acceptable service to God.

Pleasing Sacrifices

We must ask ourselves whether the Lord takes pleasure in our work. Is it pleasing to Him? Cain presented a sacrifice, but God did not look upon his sacrifice. (See Genesis 4:3–7.) We can offer God our earnestness and zeal, but the great question is whether He takes delight in us and our sacrifices.

It is not how we pray and what we do that can bring us blessing. Instead, it is the fact that God accepts our praying and doing and sends an answer to it. Many remain content when they think they have done their best to serve God and obtain rest in this duty. With living faith this is not so. It will not merely set the wood in order and slay the sacrifice, but it will also crave the fire from heaven to consume the sacrifice. (See 1 Kings 18:22–39.) Living faith desires proof that the sacrifice is pleasing and acceptable to God. Living faith does not merely seek to serve God in the way that is ordained by Him, but it also desires to know that God takes delight in its sacrifices. The tenderhearted believer must know that God is pleased with his sacrifice.

David's word teaches us further that, when God takes delight in the sacrifices of righteousness, His people also will take delight in them.

"Then shalt thou be pleased with the sacrifices of righteousness...: then shall they offer bullocks." There is nothing that will create more joyful service than the blessed certainty that God is pleased. When we know that God is pleased with our efforts and that every sacrifice is a joy to Him, our hearts become strengthened to serve Him. Sacrifice itself becomes a joy and a delight. Yes, the secret of true Christianity is the joy of knowing that God delights in our sacrifices. _"Then shall [we] offer bullocks upon thine altar."_

It will be a glorious time when, in the light of God's countenance, His people will joyfully and willingly dedicate themselves to Him. May we pray with new sincerity,

> _Do good in thy good pleasure unto Zion: build thou the walls of Jerusalem. Then shalt thou be pleased with the sacrifices of righteousness...: then shall they offer bullocks upon thine altar._ (Ps. 51:18–19)

May we always approach God with the prayer, _"Have mercy upon me, O God"_ (v. 1). May His answer strengthen us in the knowledge that God will thus deal with Zion and do good to her, and that the hour will be hastened when His church will bear the name _"Hephzibah,...for the_ LORD _delighteth in thee"_ (Isa. 62:4).